C000130081

Malayan Tales of the Yorkshire Light Infantry

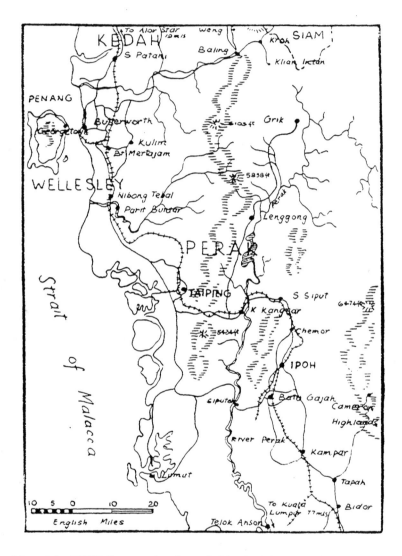

Map of the KOYLI's operational area in North Malaya, originally sketched at Battalion HQ in 1948.

Malayan Tales of
The Yorkshire Light Infantry

Presented and Edited by
John Scurr

with a Foreword by
Tom Morgan

The Pentland Press
Edinburgh – Cambridge – Durham – USA

First published in 1997 by
The Pentland Press Ltd
1 Hutton Close,
South Church
Bishop Auckland
Durham

ISBN 1-85821-475-0

Typeset by Carnegie Publishing, 18 Maynard St, Preston
Printed and bound by Antony Rowe Ltd, Chippenham

To the sounding of silver bugles
in the eager bloom of our youth,
fondly recalled in sunset's reflective glow

Contents

Contents

Illustrations

Foreword

Although these words are principally addressed to the members of our Association, I sincerely hope that other readers will also find them of interest.

When Jock asked me to contribute a story for this book, I deliberated long and hard over the many incidents I was involved in that might make a funny, sad or happy story. I have many such stories, but when I listen to some of the tales that are told at our Malaya Vets Reunions, I know that when this book is finally published, any story I could relate would pale in comparison. However, the brief anecdote that follows expresses my feelings about the early part of the Malayan "Emergency" Campaign and my part in it as a soldier of the KOYLI.

Early in 1949 the men of 3 Platoon, A Company were stumbling about in the pitch black at three o'clock in the morning on the way to set up a dawn ambush on one of the Kedah rubber estates, probably Dublin Estate. We were hopelessly lost, and had no inkling of our whereabouts. In all the ensuing confusion, Second Lieutenant Peter Sibbald – our new Platoon Commander – called out to his batman, Sid (the sadist) Winn: "Where are you, Winn?"

Out of the darkness came the reply: "How the fucking hell do I know where I am?"

This just about summed up my feelings about my unhappy involvement in the campaign so far. I hadn't slept in a bed for six months, the food was swill, we had little or no knowledge of jungle fighting, our equipment and weapons were ancient, there was no social life and we were treated like criminals most of the time. As Sid had so eloquently stated, I did not know "where the fucking hell I was" or what I was doing.

I had patrolled the jungle exhausted for days on end, looking for "invisible" bandit camps and bandits which I supposed to exist only in the fuddled mind of "Whisky Johnny" (Major Acock – Company Commander). And when we finally stumbled across them, they vanished

xiii

as if it was but a dream. The days and weeks spent marching in the blazing sun and pouring rain, sometimes settling down to sleep on the jungle "carpet" still wet through, and then returning from patrol to sleep on the floor of a wooden basha in Baling, Kroh, Klian Intan or some other godforsaken hole, passed as if it were all a horrible nightmare.

But through all this misery, one thing kept me going: the indomitable spirit of you, my fellow sufferers. You were magnificent. You helped carry my pack when I collapsed with heat exhaustion, showed me how to make a two-man bivvy and put me to bed when I was drunk. And best of all you sang with me, dragged me away from the guardroom when I was about to make a fool of myself and generally helped me to come to terms with the horrible existence that was a swaddie's lot in Malaya during those troubled times.

I will never forget your comradeship, your cheerfulness and your ability to take all they threw at you. You were trampled on, ignored and forgotten but you always came up smiling and you were always there for a mate. It was my privilege to serve with you and it is with great pride that I call myself your "mucker" .

I am sure that the stories that follow will show all of your qualities – good and bad! If anybody tells the story of me and Lucy Chong, I will sue!!

Tom Morgan
Secretary of the KOYLI Malaya Veterans Association

Introduction

A former Regular soldier who had served with two or three regiments once told me that there was something really special about the King's Own Yorkshire Light Infantry in Malaya. During that era, the 1st Battalion (originally the 2nd) KOYLI was a happy battalion, he said, with only a minimum of internal friction.

After giving this pronouncement considerable thought, I eventually concluded that there was probably a deal of truth in what he had said. Accepting that our casualties in ambushes and accidents were quite heavy and that the jungle and the climate were bastards – and so were some of the senior ranks – nonetheless our morale and comradeship were second to none, and when we were at play we got up to all kinds of mischief and laughed until the tears rolled down our cheeks. At the time, of course, most of us couldn't wait for the day when we would get to hell out of it; yet looking back today, forty-five or more years later, those of us who have survived can think of no other time in our lives that can compare with those years in Malaya for richness of experience, good and bad, or for wealth of comradeship. A happy battalion? If there is such a thing in this world as "happy", I'd say we were – though not all of the time.

My previous book *Jungle Campaign* (Owl Press, 1994) told the story of my service as a private soldier, as had been originally recorded in my Malayan journal of 1950–51, thus providing an authentic and detailed account of everyday life in the Battalion at that time. The book also contained a potted history of the 2nd and 1st Battalions in Malaya and described in as much detail as was available to me every encounter with the enemy that I could find on record and the deaths of all of our fallen comrades.

This second book is not intended to be a history of the KOYLI in Malaya. It is simply a collection of soldiers' stories, told by the men who lived them, including a few yarns of my own which I had omitted from *Jungle Campaign* in order to limit that book to a reasonable length. Nonetheless, I have placed the stories in as near to chronological order

1

as I have been able to ascertain and the end result could possibly be regarded as some kind of "living history".

There are one or two statements in a couple of the stories which do not tally with the official records. I have neither altered nor indicated these for two reasons. Firstly, I know from my own researches into various subjects over the years that records are not always correct. And secondly, I am not going to dispute a point with someone who was there when I was not. It is also evident that some stories, describing the same incident, appear to contradict one another. This is fairly normal with eyewitness accounts of dramatic events. Although such differences can be confusing I find that they merely add to the interest and fascination of these splendid tales.

I am very grateful to all of the contributors for the excellent accounts they have provided of their personal experiences during those years. (It should be noted that the ranks stated are those that were held by the contributors at the time of their stories, irrespective of any promotions later achieved.) I should also like to thank Redvers Battersby, Raymond Bays, Roy Caldecott, Sid Grant, Gordon Hill, "Hutch" Hutchinson, Frank Keenan, John Kitchen, Ivor Lewis, Tom Morgan, Peter Peace, Ron Stringer and George Williams for kindly making photographs available to me from their private collections.

Very briefly, the historical background to the stories is as follows :

The 2nd Battalion, King's Own Yorkshire Light Infantry arrived in Malaya from India on 29 September 1947. At that time, Communist subversion was rife in many parts of the world and no more so than in Malaya where the Malayan Communist Party's campaign of murder and intimidation led to the declaration of a State of Emergency by the British High Commissioner on 16 June 1948. The Communist terrorists – eventually calling themselves the Malayan Races Liberation Army – were mainly Chinese and were universally known as "bandits" during the early years of the Emergency. However, they were in fact a uniformed, well organised and comparatively well armed guerrilla army, though their weaponry was often badly affected by jungle rot.

On 18 November 1948 the 2nd Battalion was converted into the 1st Battalion, KOYLI. The Battalion's operational area normally comprised of the southern half of Kedah, Province Wellesley and Perak, with headquarters on the Island of Penang.

1. Men of C Company in Taiping camp in 1948, looking far from happy.

The heaviest casualties suffered by the Battalion were in enemy ambushes; namely, at Bidor on 2 October 1948 when one officer and three other ranks of B Company were killed and three ORs were wounded; on the Kroh-Klian Intan road on 3 December 1949 when four ORs of B Company were killed and one wounded; and at Ampang on 10 June 1950 when six ORs of D Company were killed and four wounded, one of whom died six days later.

The Battalion's biggest successes occurred at Karangan on 11 January 1949 when a patrol of seven men of D Company killed all of a party of five bandits; at Lubok Segintah on 6 June 1949 when a Platoon of B Company surprised and killed four bandits and captured one in a dawn raid; and at Anak Kulim on 9 November 1949 when a patrol of D Company fought off a numerically superior force, killing two bandits for sure and almost certainly another six for the loss of one KOYLI private killed. There were several other well-fought actions in which bandits were killed in small numbers by all of the companies, and in which there were small but nonetheless greatly lamented KOYLI losses.

On 7 August 1951 the 1st Battalion, KOYLI sailed for home on HMT *Dunera*, leaving behind two officers and thirty-three other ranks who had lost their lives; one officer and seventeen ORs killed in action and one officer and sixteen ORs dead from accidents and disease. At the time of the Battalion's return to the UK the official figure of bandits killed by the KOYLI during the Malayan tour was declared to be thirty-four. How this figure was arrived at I do not know, but simple arithmetic has persuaded me that thirty-nine enemy personnel were killed for sure by KOYLI patrols and possibly as many as forty-six or even more.

It is interesting to note that in the thirty-seven months from the beginning of the Emergency in June 1948 to when the Battalion left Malaya, thirty-three bandits were killed by the KOYLI during the first twenty months and only six during the last seventeen months. This wide proportional difference is made all the more remarkable when you consider that far more bandits were being killed in Malaya as a whole during the later period than during the earlier one. I don't believe there can be any explanation for this, other than sheer lack of luck during the later period.

The paradox of the KOYLI in Malaya experience was succinctly expressed in a letter I recently received from Australia, in which my old friend from those days, Signals Corporal Arthur Greenacre, stated: "All I can say is that I was glad when the three years were completed – but I would not have missed it for the world. It was an experience that I feel privileged to have been a part of."

Here, then, are the Malayan tales of "the Happy(?) Battalion."

John (Jock) Scurr, 1996

1.

Flo by Moonlight

Ted Slade – Private MT Platoon

While serving in India, I was transferred from the Somerset Light Infantry to the KOYLI and duly arrived in Malaya with the 2nd Battalion in September 1947. In our barracks in Taiping there were some sports facilities and there were a few cinemas and other places of amusement in the town, but there was shortly discovered a special, secret entertainment that was enjoyed by those in the know in HQ Company.

Serjeant Gilpin was married to a black Tamil woman called Flo. Although of a heavy build, she was quite attractive and had a large and beautiful bust. Now it so happened that Serjeant Gilpin's home in the Married Quarters stood just opposite the fuel point by the back gate of the camp, and this fuel point was guarded by a prowling sentry. However, around 10 pm the sentry was always nowhere to be seen. The reason for this was that he had climbed up into the rafters over the fuel pump in order to get a better view of a window in the house opposite.

Every night, Flo would stand at that window, leisurely brushing her long black hair, with her lovely big tits poking forward, straining to get out of her flimsy silk blouse. Oh my! It was a sight worth climbing for and a sight worth waiting for.

Fortunately, Flo never spotted any of her nightly succession of clandestine admirers, and for months guard duty at the fuel point remained something to look forward to.

2.

Early Days at Taiping

George Williams – Private B Company

Late in 1947 I was posted to the 2nd Battalion, Durham Light Infantry at Singapore. Soon after arrival, however, some of the lads were told that they would be going home with the Colours while the rest of us were informed that we would be joining the 2nd Battalion, KOYLI, stationed at a place called Taiping.

What a journey we had in that hard-seated, shaking train with a wood-burning loco! We were thankful to arrive at Taiping where we found that nearly all the camp buildings had tin roofs. The first order we were given was to put our kit down and fall in. That was when we met CSM Crossland, known as "Togo". Someone said he was Acting RSM at that time. When he reached my place in the line, he put his nose almost to mine and snarled: "You can take that fucking cap badge down!"

He meant my DLI badge and, as ordered, I later had to put the KOYLI badge in its place. I thought to myself – I joined the Durhams because my brother served with them in Burma and now they've put me in this mob! But I realised that a lot of Durhams were with me and that I'd have to try to make the best of it.

In the weeks that followed, we did the usual training, weapons and marching, but no jungle training. As an antidote to malaria I took my daily mepacrine tablet which soon turned me a nice yellow colour. Then there was salt parade, with the choice of a concentrated salt tablet or a pint of salt water. I favoured the latter as I found that the tablets burned my guts.

Colonel Hickie was at that time Battalion CO. With a few others I was allocated to 6 Platoon, B Company. Our OC was Major Bell, Fletcher was our CSM and Price our CQMS. My first task with 6 Platoon was to manhandle a jeep and trailer into a Dakota aircraft. Then, about thirty-two strong, we flew with these vehicles to Kota Bahru. I noticed the railway and the road below looked about half an

6

2. Private George Williams (left) with two other B Company men, displaying a trophy from a bandit camp. Lenggong, 1948.

inch wide and fervently hoped that the bottom wouldn't fall out of the plane.

Shortly after that, RSM Monument (and he looked like one!) arrived in Taiping. One day, CSM Fletcher was taking a parade when someone dropped his rifle. Fletcher threw his beret up in the air and when it came down he stamped on it. Then he knelt down and shouted: "For God's sake, send me some fucking soldiers!" At that, RSM Monument stepped forward, fuming, and ordered Fletcher off the square.

CSM "Togo" Crossland now replaced Fletcher in B Company. On parade, Togo was inspecting the front rank and stopped opposite an older soldier who was two places past me. The old soldier looked Togo in the eye and said: "That was a fucking long shit you had!" He explained to us afterwards that, while in Burma in 1944, Togo had gone for a shit just before the Japs had overrun their position and this was the first time he had seen him since!

Then patrolling started – months before the Emergency was official. On a jungle operation in the Lenggong region in April 1948, Major Bell, CQMS Price and Private Foley were trying to obtain some form of shelter during a heavy rainstorm. A tree rolled upon them, killing

7

Price and Foley. Major Bell was very badly injured; I think his back was broken. He was placed on poncho-capes and carried over the river. MT driver Cadwallader drove him to hospital. I don't know to this day whether he lived or died.

These were the first of B Company's many casualties.

3.

The Captain's Challenge

James Harper – Private KOYLI Draft

It was the summer of 1948. We were on a troopship somewhere in the Indian Ocean, bound for Singapore. By now, the troops were becoming dull and uninterested through being cooped up and were longing for land which was still a few days away.

In an attempt to relieve the boredom, our troopdeck officer, a Captain, decided to have a boxing ring erected. Then he assembled all the troops around the ring and coolly stepped inside, dressed in his PT kit (vest and shorts). His vest was adorned with ABA insignia, indicating that he had boxed for the Army. So he was no fool. He then held up a pair of boxing gloves and issued a challenge to the crowd. There were no takers.

So, in an act of mock defiance, the Captain threw the gloves into the crowd where they landed in the lap of Private Bob Raynor. Bob, in his very broad Nottinghamshire accent, indicated that he did not wish to participate, but he was finally goaded into accepting the challenge. Quite calmly, he put on the gloves, stepped into the ring and proceeded to give the Captain a severe thrashing around the body, thereby breaking three of the officer's ribs.

In Malaya, Bob was posted to A Company. He served in the Battalion for four years; then joined the Durhams for Korea. He was quite a lad!

4.

A Loveable Scamp

Redvers Battersby – Provost Corporal HQ Company

When the 2nd Battalion was transferred from Taiping to Penang in May 1948, I was with the last batch to leave Taiping camp as I had to hand over the guardroom to the Malay Regiment's Police. I duly arrived in Glugor Barracks, Penang, and took over the guardroom there from the West Yorkshire Regimental Police who were with their Battalion's rear party.

The West Yorkshire RPs showed me round and their Provost Corporal said to me finally: "You see this monkey? Well, he's our pet. We're going home, so we can't take him with us and I don't want to give him to the locals. He's house trained and he's also trained to fetch a coconut down any time you want one. If you take him, he'll give you no trouble. His name is Monty."

At that moment, the monkey was sitting quietly and seemed well behaved, so I agreed to take him over. I was billeted in a bungalow at the back of the guardroom, so I kept Monty there until the West Yorkshires left and he got used to me. Everywhere I went he followed me like a dog, and he was a favourite with all the lads when they found he would get coconuts for them from the palm trees.

It was after about a month when Monty started his antics. First of all, he shut the dhobi girls in my room one day and wouldn't let them out. I was in the guardroom when I heard the girls screaming so I had to go and rescue them, and the result was that I had to bring my dhobi to the guardroom if I wanted it done.

It was not long after that when Monty began to display what became a regular habit. When I was checking someone in camp and the soldier in question was stood to attention before me, Monty would sneak up behind him, put a hand up his shorts and try to pull one of the hairs off the man's testicles! You can imagine what it was like with me shouting: "Keep still!" and Monty creating havoc. It was the same when

9

3. Provost Corporal Redvers Battersby (left) with Lance Corporal Watson of the Regimental Police. Penang, 1948.

the defaulters were on parade. Anyway, eventually the lads got fed up with this and decided on action.

The defaulters always got an hour at night, nine to ten, to go to the NAAFI, a large building at the top of the hill from the guardroom. Monty was a favourite in the NAAFI at night and the lads occasionally gave him a drink. This particular night, a few of the lads in the NAAFI met up with the defaulters and carried out their plot. They gave Monty all the Tiger beer he wanted and he was soon blind drunk.

But what followed took everyone by surprise. Monty went on the rampage and completely smashed up the NAAFI. He chased all the Chinese staff and soldiers out, throwing anything that came to hand – bottles full and empty, glasses, Brasso, boot polish, sweets, chocolate, cakes, the lot. He simply went berserk and cleared the NAAFI in half an hour flat. The place was in a shambles by the time I was sent for.

When I arrived on the scene, Monty was in the NAAFI on his own, still throwing stuff at the walls. I opened the door and shouted: "Monty! Get your arse out here!"

He took one look at me and bolted past me through the door into the night. It was the following day before he came back to the bungalow, and what a state he was in! He was still woozy and covered in foot powder, boot polish, Brasso, etc.

Anyway, the outcome was that nobody was charged with getting him drunk but I was ordered to get rid of him and not allow him back into camp.

So I sold Monty to the contractor who collected the coconuts in the surrounding area for twenty dollars and had a good drink on him. Many a time afterwards, I saw Monty working among the palm trees on the end of a long lead. I couldn't recognise him, as one monkey is the same as another at a distance. But he always knew me and scampered over to give me a hug. He was really a loveable scamp.

5.

Thank God!

Ivor Lewis – Corporal Signal Platoon

Having been posted to the 2nd Battalion, KOYLI, I arrived in Penang in May 1948. It would appear that post-war army units had been restructured into smaller formations. This may have made strategic sense, but to the general swaddie meant a shortage of personnel for most jobs that had to be done in all units. This particularly translated into everyone having to do more than the average number of guard duties.

On arrival at Glugor Barracks, I was immediately grabbed for duty as Guard Commander and transported to the ammunition dump (generally known as "the magazine") which was located at the rear of the barrack complex, near to the MT pool. I was greeted there by Corporal Jock McClung who was sporting a stubble of beard growth. His opening comments were: "Thank God they've sent somebody to relieve me! I thought I was going to be stuck here for ever!" He proceeded to hand over his pistol and then promptly disappeared before I had time to gather my thoughts.

I managed to glean some information from the existing sentries regarding what we were supposed to be guarding, and I was not

11

particularly enthused to learn that the ammunition dump was reputed to be haunted by a murdered Japanese patrol!

All went without undue incident until darkness fell upon the camp. I was casually leaning against the outside wall of the guardroom when I noticed a strange light approaching me. Without hesitation I withdrew my pistol from its holster and pointed it in the general direction of the light. As it drew nearer, I called out: "Halt! Who goes there?"

There was no reply and my visitor drew even closer. I now demanded excitedly: "Halt, or I fire!" At which point the light buzzed past the barrel of my pistol, giving me quite a fright. My mind raced to an apparition of the Japanese patrol, but it turned out to be merely my first encounter with a Malayan firefly! It must have been only inches away from me when I first challenged it!

Despite this rational outcome, the possibility of ghostly encounters was now firmly planted in my mind. When I eventually completed my first guard duty at the ammunition dump, my first words to the relieving Guard Commander were: "Thank God they've sent somebody to relieve me!"

6.

On the Nose

Ted Slade – Private MT Platoon

Battalion HQ moved from Taiping to Glugor Barracks, Penang in May 1948. Although there was little terrorist activity on the island, I nonetheless always had to be armed while carrying out my duties as a dispatch rider. Rather than hump my rifle around, I regularly used to borrow Signals Corporal Dixon's revolver.

One day when returning for tiffen, I drove up the ramp into the MT shed and parked my motorbike. Private "Muscles" Curry was sitting on a charpoy (bed) as I unloaded my revolver close by. Satisfied all bullets were removed, I slammed the chamber shut and pressed the trigger. Bang! A protesting shout drew my eyes towards Muscles who was holding his nose with blood running all over the place. The bullet had fortunately only nicked the tip of his nose, but it didn't half bleed!

4. Privates Ted Slade (right) and "Pedro" Pinchbeck of the MT Section at the Hotel Metropole in Georgetown, 1948.

Lieutenant Moore, the MTO, then came running in, followed by an MT lance corporal. I quickly grabbed up an inner tube and told the Lieutenant I'd had a blowout. In the meanwhile, Muscles had very obligingly turned the other way, covering up the bleeding as best he could. Lieutenant Moore gave me a suspicious look but, to my relief, then turned and walked out.

It was an accident that could have been a tragedy if the trajectory of the bullet had been just a couple of inches inward but, as it was, it became quite a joke in the MT Platoon.

7.

Fanny To Windward

Roy Caldecott – Private KOYLI Draft

'Twas on the good ship "Windrush" in August 1948. Arthur Greenacre and I were standing by the ship's rail, watching the muck and rubbish being churned up from the harbour bottom as the ship pulled away from the wharf. England was slowly shrinking as Southampton lay in the ship's wake. We had been allocated our troopdeck along with a troopdeck Sergeant from the Buffs Regiment – five feet, four inches of monster who was screaming to be five feet, five inches. No matter what we did or how we did it, it was always wrong.

It happened to be our first day in the Bay of Biscay when I found myself on guard (can you believe it?) – 1st deck, station 1 for'ard. Standing at my post, feeling and probably looking a little green, I was approached by an aged marine who seemed a little tipsy.

"Don't you feel well?" were his first words.

"Not too bad thanks, mate," I answered, trying to be friendly.

"Look for'ard," he ordered. "When that point goes down and the bows disappear into a wave, breathe in. And when it comes up, breathe out. At night when you're in your bunk, sleep with your head towards the bows. When your head goes down, breathe in. And when it comes up, breathe out. You must learn to live with the ship, get into the rhythm. It'll help you to sleep."

This seemed reasonable to me, so I tried it and it worked. (Thank you, I say now to the aged marine.) I never felt ill again. In fact, I went looking for it whenever we hit bad weather.

We had in our draft two corporals who had seen a bit of army life – Roy (Nobby) Clarke, who was a Canadian, and Bill Baines. They both brought a little sanity to our trip. When we had traversed the Med, which compared with the Bay was like floating over a mirror, the Red Sea was an education. But now the ship was entering the Indian Ocean and another storm.

On board we had some ladies and children who were on their way

14

East to join their husbands and fathers. One lady would always stand in the same place every time she was on deck, the deck above the one on which I had done my guard duty. She always wore shorts and always faced the wind whichever direction it came from. She became an everyday attraction, weather permitting.

One hell of a storm was now long past and we were approaching Ceylon, looking forward to stretching our sea legs on solid ground in Colombo. By this time, our troopdeck Buffs Sergeant had become quite amenable, in fact rather friendly. After leaving Ceylon, Arthur and I were on deck talking to Nobby and Bill. We asked them about the change in our troopdeck Sergeant's attitude.

Nobby said: "There is a rumour going around that during the storm in the Indian Ocean, someone held the Sergeant by his ankles over the side of the ship and gave him the option of mending his ways or having a bath!"

The rest of our journey to Singapore was thus more enjoyable.

On reaching Singapore, I once again found myself on duty; this time, baggage duty. We had to bring from the cabins luggage marked "Not Wanted on Voyage". This was the extra baggage brought on board by the married parties. After bringing out a large trunk on my two-wheeled conveyance and placing it near a rope-netting device for slinging onto the dock, I looked around. There stood the lady, still wearing the wide-legged shorts and facing the gentle breeze.

Two crewmen were nearby. "Do you know the lady?" asked one.

"No," I answered. "Not even her name."

"We call her Fanny," he said. "Fanny to Windward."

Very apt, I thought.

8.

My Luckiest Day

Frank Keenan – Private B Company

There were a lot of good lads in the KOYLI in Malaya – a lot of brave young men I thought very highly of. I later saw active service in Kenya, Cyprus and Borneo, and the lads with me there were just as brave, but there will always be a special place in my heart for the Malaya lads of 1948–51.

The luckiest day of my life was 2 October 1948 when I was in 4 Platoon, B Company. The previous day we had been on patrol near Bidor and found this beautiful waterfall with two pools; one deep and one shallow. Captain Lock said: "Anyone who can swim – in the big pool. If you can't – in the small one." He then put out sentries and the rest of us stripped off our gear. I could swim, so I got in the deep pool and we all enjoyed a good swim in the cool water.

Next day, it was planned to do the same again, only this time we were going to fire on the range first. I should have gone as Private Buckland's Number Two on the Bren gun and was loading up magazines when Private Ridden asked me what I was doing. I told him that Captain Lock had ordered me to go as Buckland's Number Two.

Ridden was Buckland's friend, so he said to me: "No you don't. I'm going."

I told him to see Captain Lock about it, which he did.

Then, Captain Lock came to me and said: "Keenan, stay behind as room orderly." So that was that.

Later on, we heard the sound of firing twice and thought the lads were still on the range. Then, two soldiers came running in, both wounded, and said the boys had been ambushed in the jungle pool. We all jumped on the trucks and got out there as fast as we could. The bodies were all over the place. It was a terrible sight.

I still thank my lucky stars for that escape. If I had gone that day, I probably wouldn't have been writing this now.

9.

Ambush at Bidor

George Williams – Private B Company

In the ambush at the Bidor quarry pool on 2 October 1948, the lads were bathing in the water when the bandits opened fire. Captain Lock, Lance Corporal Hutchinson and Privates Dobson and Woodhouse were killed, and Privates Hawksworth, Ridden and Buckland were wounded.

5. Privates Lyons, Wooding and Joe Sidoli (left to right, front row) just back from patrol with 6 Platoon, B Company in 1949.

I was back in camp when this happened. As soon as we heard the shooting, we all hurried from the camp site to the pool while firing was still going on. But we got there just a few seconds too late.

Captain Lock, we were told, had forty-two wounds in his body. I saw Buckland put his finger in a bullet-wound to try to stop it from bleeding. Our lads had opened up at the bandits on the quarry face and killed one. Joe Sidoli scaled the quarry and grabbed a wounded bandit. Then, lifting him high over his head, Joe threw him onto the rocks below, killing the bastard. Well, everyone in B Company was really mad at what had happened and couldn't wait to set out after the bandits.

On 16 October, after having gone for miles and miles through the jungle, we suddenly came upon them. The leading scout spotted a bandit washing in a stream. As the bandit looked up, Private Kelly gave him a full mag from his Bren gun. The bandit jumped a sort of dance as he was hit with thirty-two rounds of . 303. When we passed his body, I noticed a round had gone sideways round his neck and seemed to have burned a collar under his skin. The next bandit we saw ran out of a nearby basha. Corporal Flint, who was just in front of me, gave him a full Sten mag. I saw the bullets strike the bandit from his right

17

hip across his chest and left shoulder, but he still managed to turn and run off into the jungle. We found his body later.

In the basha we found bombs, guns and rifle butts that the bandits had been making. You could see pin-holes through the sides of the barrels. All told, it had been a good result for 6 Platoon and we'd got some of our own back for the lads of 4 Platoon who'd been killed in the pool.

After we got back to camp, we were dismayed to find ourselves put on 15-cwts and 3-tonners and then dropped off in threes at extended intervals with orders to ambush the fifty bandits who were supposed to be coming along the track (but didn't). I won't mention some of the comments that were made!

10.

A Damn Good Job

John Storey – Private B Company

I think we did a damn good job protecting the plantation owners in Malaya. We were under risk of ambush all the time and what we did was definitely underestimated by people at home.

It was a sad time in October 1948 when I lost my pal Woodhouse who was killed in the jungle swimming pool at Bidor, along with Captain Lock and the others. They never got out of the pool. There were two men on guard but they were outnumbered.

After that, B Company became more forceful. A couple of weeks later, we got word from local Sakais that the Communists had a camp in the jungle nearby. So we approached under cover of darkness and surprised them as dawn was breaking. I was Number Two on the Bren. Some of them were shaving in the stream with their Sten guns and rifles beside them, but they didn't get the chance to use them. We opened up with rapid fire. Bodies and steel mirrors were soon lying awash in the stream.

The rest of them fled. In their camp they had been making an armoury, and we brought back a lot of weapons and ammo. That day, I was also driving a Canadian Dodge, carrying eight men, as the Company was short of drivers.

We were ambushed a few times which wasn't very nice. One day at Kroh, near the border, we went to pick up fresh drinking-water and were fired upon from one side of the road. I put my foot down on the accelerator but nearly lost control, and the water in the tank was all over the place. But the second driver and myself got safely back to camp.

On our few leaves in Georgetown, Penang, we had a lot of fun. We spent all day in restaurants having good meals and putting records on, and also shopping for bargains. At night, me and John Peel would get in a trishaw and head for the City Lights dance hall. We'd go in and buy a big book of tickets to dance with the hostess-girls. One night, we never got there. I fell in the trishaw and burned my arm on the oil lamp. John Peel filled the driver in and I had to stop him. By that time, the Redcaps had arrived and they put us both inside for the night.

In the guardhouse I met a Regular soldier who was a really bad case – always absent on parade and going missing in Georgetown. On this table he had nailed three wire strings and was playing a tune on them with a razor-blade while singing in a quiet voice. He also used to drink meths when he got fed up with the Army.

Sadly, I've forgotten a lot of things that happened in those days, but I sometimes think of the egg and bacon banjos (sandwiches) we got from the char wallah and the times on leave when we went swimming from Sandycroft beach and fishing from the huts the Malays had in the sea. Then there was the convalescence camp in the Cameron Highlands, high up in the mountains. It was a terrible drive up but the air was lovely. We had big sports days in Penang when we won cups and medals. I played football for the Battalion on certain days against fast Chinese teams.

Apart from when Sir Henry Gurney, the High Commissioner, was ambushed and killed, there wasn't much in the press about the campaign in Malaya. We should have been mentioned more for the commendable part we played in defeating Communism.

11.

Bugles, Mortars and Tent Pegs

Joe Wrigglesworth – Private Bugle Platoon

I joined the 2nd Battalion in Penang in October 1948, having sailed to Malaya with the regimental band aboard the troopship *Devonshire*. On arrival at Glugor Barracks, I was immediately posted to the Bugle Platoon which was commanded by Bugle Major Bert Harbisher, MM. Most of the buglers I already knew from when we were stationed at Minden in Germany during 1946–47. The rest were two or three 2nd Battalion buglers and a few lads who were new to the Platoon.

The 1st Battalion, KOYLI had disbanded between December 1947 and April 1948 at Plymouth. I remember distinctly that from my arrival in Penang, the regimental call of the 2nd Battalion was sounded by the duty bugler until the amalgamation took place and the unit title was officially changed to 1st Battalion.

During the next three years, the Bugle Platoon performed various tasks. We had to provide a duty bugler for Glugor Barracks, later renamed Minden Barracks. Another of our specialities was tent erecting. We learned that job early on and became experts at it. Whenever the Battalion wanted some tents to be erected and we were available, we were sent for. On operational duty we were the Defence Platoon. Sometimes our role was similar to that of the rifle platoons.

In between all that, we went on ceremonial parades with the band. One parade I remember especially was when the Battalion provided a guard of honour for HMS *Amethyst* during that ship's visit to Penang in September 1949.

Our most outstanding task commenced in 1949 when it was decided that the Bugle Platoon would, in addition to its other duties, become the Mortar Platoon. We were issued with 3-inch mortars and began a training course in our own barracks in Penang. We soon became proficient and thereafter, whenever the Battalion required the support of 3-inch mortars, we provided it. In addition to mortars we were also trained in the use of flame-throwers.

Some of the buglers were keen sportsmen and played in both rugby and soccer teams. Corporal Ken Stanhope played rugby for the Battalion and also for Penang. Jim Gardner was a keen soccer player and played for both the HQ Company and Battalion teams. In our free time we all enjoyed visits to Georgetown, particularly at weekends.

As time went by and one after the other, some of the Platoon left for the UK, the number of trained buglers was much depleted. Those departed were replaced by enthusiastic trainees but it was a long and patient process to become a proficient bugler from scratch.

My recollections of Malaya would not be complete without writing a few words about Bugle Major Bert Harbisher, MM, BEM. As I write these notes, I have received word that sadly he has passed away. He was a real soldier in every respect and a good bugle major.

In conclusion, I would like to say that all in the Bugle Platoon were a great bunch of lads to serve with and their comradeship was second to none. In early August 1951, we left Penang with the rest of the Battalion aboard the troopship *Dunera* to return home to the UK.

12.

Night Alert

Gordon Cadwallader – Private MT Platoon

In 1948 I was attached to A Company and at that time we were camped around a police station in a village near Ipoh, the name of which I cannot remember.

One night at dusk, we were just settled down when we heard the sound of shots in the distance. So we were put on immediate alert. Then, the phone rang in the police station and someone on the line said he was calling from Batu Gajah Police Station and that they were under attack and needed help. But our Company Commander, Major Bob Armistead, said that the Security Forces normally did not phone each other but kept in touch by wireless. When Batu Gajah was then contacted, the police there said they were being sniped at but could cope and did not need help. The call had obviously been a ruse to draw the

21

Company out into a waiting ambush, so we doubled the guard and the rest of us stood down.

Some time later when it was really dark, we came under fire and returned fire ourselves. The action went on for about half an hour and then suddenly stopped. Out attackers then began to shout at us to come out and find them. We had more sense and everything soon went quiet and settled down.

Later on, one of the lads was taken ill with stomach pains and the MI orderly said he should go to hospital in Ipoh. They put the lad in the back of a 3-tonner and I led the way in my 30-cwt with an escort. It was pretty scary, wondering if the terrorists were still out there waiting for us. But we made it to Ipoh and back OK with no further sign of them.

13.

Ill Met on the Border

Redvers Battersby – Corporal D Company

On an operation near the Siam border in 1948, all three platoons of D Company were converging on a village. I was a corporal in 11 Platoon. Second Lieutenant Wigg was Platoon Commander and Chadwick was Platoon Serjeant. We understood that all Malayan forces – police and local Home Guards – knew we were in the area. We were delayed in getting to the village due to the fact that our maps only showed roads and plantations; the rest was marked as uncharted jungle.

Although it was growing dark, it was decided to press on. We got onto a decent track and determined to use it as it was going in the right direction. About a quarter of a mile down the track, one of the lads saw a movement just off the track and fired at it, shouting: "Ambush!"

Everybody dropped and all hell broke loose, with everyone firing into the undergrowth. After about three minutes (which seemed like an hour) I noticed there was no return fire, so I shouted: "Cease fire!" and crawled back to Mr Wigg. The moon was coming up, so he decided we should remain in the stand-to position until it was light enough to see.

After half an hour, with the moon up like it was daylight and everybody still edgy, it was decided to go and investigate where the movement had been seen. The Platoon closed up; then four men crawled forward and found a Malay Special Constable dead against a slit-trench. A few yards to the left was another trench with two Malays crouched in the bottom. They were dragged out and brought to the track. It transpired later that the police were in an ambush position along the track in slit-trenches and had got settled in. The one who was shot was the look-out. Apparently, he was their company's best shot and had won prizes for his shooting. When the firing had started, the rest of them all got down, too frightened to move, until we rounded them up.

Later at the Civil Court, Second Lieutenant Wigg and the rest of us were found not guilty of homicide and the widow was paid compensation for which she thanked Serjeant Chadwick. That luck stayed with me all through the time I was in Malaya.

14.

Squelch!

Roy Caldecott – Lance Corporal A Company

We were under canvas late in 1948. Tronoh springs to mind but it could have been anywhere. At the time, A Company had some HQ Company personnel as our guests, and three of us decided to go to the AKC cinema show that evening – myself, Bugler Stanhope and one other. The afternoon had seen a convoy of gharries churning up what little of a road the camp had, dropping off this and that here and there and picking up those married men who were to be taken to Penang to join their families for the weekend – known eventually as the Passion Parade!

The gharries had left behind about two feet, maybe three, of mud in troughs and trenches. The last hour had seen an outburst of rain and the three of us, sheltering under a tent-flap watching the troughs and trenches fill up, knew that the mire would have to be crossed twice, as the gharries had gone round in circles, before we could get to the film. Even so, we made the mud-spattered trip to the AKC. Then, the film

23

over, we decided to have a nightcap in the NAAFI tent, only to find that the NAAFI had been closed early by the RSM due to a shortage of customers. This did not please us at all and uttering one blasphemy after another, the three of us linked up arm-in-arm ready to brave the return crossing of the mire.

Suddenly, Bugler Stanhope sneezed and out shot his dentures – a plate with two teeth attached. Where the molars landed was anyone's guess. How near or how far were we to start a search?

"I'm on duty tomorrow," said Stanhope, "and I can't blow Reveille without my teeth!"

The night being black with a tropical storm teaming down, we dropped to our knees and started the search from our toes forwards. Squelch! said the mud as it was squeezed through our fingers. Squelch! said my right foot as I tried to get it to follow the left. Squelch! Squelch! to left and right as the three of us moved slowly forward.

I say to the reader: put your mind to picturing yourself being out in that black, tropical thunderstorm, squelching with every step taken, and coming across three sober swaddies on hands and knees, laughing their heads off, and upon enquiring what the three were doing, being answered: "Looking for two false teeth!" I leave it to your good imagination and ask you also to be kind, as I was one of that trio!

I forget now who did find the offending molars but find them we did. At one of our recent KOYLI Malaya Veterans Reunions, forty-five or more years later, I was passed a small parcel of a serviette. I opened up the serviette only to find inside a denture-plate with two teeth attached. On looking down the row of faces to my left from which direction the parcel had come, my eyes stopped at a face with a gap in the mouth where two teeth should have been. Are these the same ones? I mimed to the gap; to which the gap nodded back in reply – yes. Pass them back – I was made to understand from the frantic gestures. Not on your life! I mimed back to the gap. Then I wrote on a slip of paper: "These are on their way to the Regimental Museum!"

I'm glad Stanhope can still take a joke. After a shake of hands and a couple of Tigers, he was once again reunited with his renowned plate. It's really saying something for army-made teeth not to have worn out after forty-odd years!

15.

Not Guilty

Redvers Battersby – Corporal D Company

I first palled up with Jack Smeaton in India and continued to serve
alongside him in Malaya. He was a quiet, unassuming bloke when
sober; butter wouldn't melt in his mouth. But what a character when
he'd had a few drinks! When he was drunk and on the rampage down
town, the MPs used to look for me as I was the only one who could
get him back into camp without any further trouble. As Provost Corporal, I used to put him in the cells and make sure he was back in bed
before Reveille.

When I left the Regimental Police and joined D Company, Jack was
Bren-gunner in my Section. One day on the Caledonia Estate towards
the end of 1948, someone going on guard duty overlooking the river
took Jack's LMG without telling him. About an hour later, the Serjeant
Major came boiling into my tent shouting for Smeaton. Jack soon turned
up, asking: "What's up?"

"Get dressed. You're on Company Orders," the CSM answered. And
then to me: "You are as well."

Off we went to the Company Office. "Caps off! Quick march!" In
we went. On the table in front of us stood Jack's Bren gun. The charge
against me – not checking all sentry positions; against Jack – leaving
his post and his Bren.

I denied the charge and said that I was no longer on duty, having
come off guard and handed over to another NCO. So my charge was
dismissed.

Then the Company Commander asked Jack: "Is this your Bren gun?"

Jack looked at it and said: "Yes, sir."

"Why have you left your post?"

"Because I'm not on guard, sir. I was on last night with Corporal
Battersby."

"Then what was your Bren doing at the river post?"

"I don't know, sir," Jack answered. "But them who borrowed it while

25

I was having a shower would have had a shock if they'd been attacked, as that mag what's on it is empty and I've got the working parts in my pocket!"

"Case dismissed!" – And a certain NCO who brought the charges found himself in hot water!

This was probably the only time that Jack was found not guilty. When in Penang, he was always in trouble through too much beer and in the end the Company Commander, Major "Porky" Gowans, issued an order banning him from setting foot on Penang Island! So when the Company went in for refit, Jacky was transferred to another company. He was the only soldier in the British Army not allowed on Penang Island. And the Battalion carried out the order to the letter.

16.

The Colonel's Surprise

James Harper – Private D Company

1949 had not long dawned and two corporals knocking back "the Tiger" in the NAAFI in Glugor Barracks, Penang were beginning to get merry. The two NCOs were worlds apart in their outlook on life. One, a Yorkshireman, was a pre-war soldier with three campaign medal ribbons on his chest – the Africa Star, Italy Star and France/Germany Star. He had been in Malaya for about a year and was the Colonel's batman.

The other was a much younger soldier. Having joined up in 1945, he had just qualified for the War Medal. However, he had since seen active service in Palestine with the KSLI, earning him the General Service Medal with Palestine clasp. Before he was 21, he had been promoted to Sergeant but was forced to relinquish his third tape on his return to England in late 1947/early 1948. This corporal was a Canadian called Roy (Nobby) Clarke and he was now becoming widely known in the KOYLI. Because of his Western, Canadian drawl, he stuck out like a sore thumb and was regularly engaged in conversation.

The evening wore on and by NAAFI closing time, the Colonel's batman was well and truly plastered and absolutely incapable. There was no alternative than to carry him back to his bunk which was in the Officers' Mess; that imposing, palatial residence which was situated well away from the barrack complex. Undaunted, Nobby proceeded on his arduous journey, bearing his heavy load. After stealthily entering the Officers' Mess, he got to within feet of the Colonel's batman's bunk when he was hailed by none other than Colonel Brown who had been disturbed by some accidental noise.

"What is the trouble?" the Colonel's voice enquired into the darkness.

Back from that darkness came a Canadian drawl: "It's your batman, sir. He's drunk – as drunk as a goddammed Indian!"

17.

A Desperate Last Stand

This was the report made by Serjeant T R Chadwick, following an action fought by seven men of 11 Platoon, D Company near Karangan on 11 January 1949. Serjeant Chadwick was subsequently awarded the MM.

We had just come out of an estate clearing where rubber trees had been cut down when we suddenly saw the five bandits. They were walking along the bank of a river about forty yards in front of us. They dived down behind the bank, at the same time opening fire at our leading scout.

We quickly sought cover ourselves and returned fire. One bandit was hit and his dead body floated down the stream. However, the bandits had the advantage of superior cover. Although we were firing downhill at them, they presented only a small target. Luckily for us, they kept popping out to take pot shots at us. Soon, we were able to kill another one. All this time we had been gradually moving down towards their position, but we had to be very careful as each time any one of us exposed himself, we drew a hail of bullets from the terrorists.

After the encounter had gone on for fifteen minutes, one of the bandits threw a grenade. It fell short and rolled down into the stream. Eventually we cornered another bandit who tried to jump over a fence.

6. Men of D Company proudly display their captured Communist flag, following a successful action at the outset of 1949.

As he jumped we fired and he fell dead. Only the girl and one armed bandit were left.

The girl had been hit but would not give up. To enable her companion to refill his rifle, she went on firing with her pistol. I then decided to leave two men on the hill and get the rest down so that they could creep up on the bandits and take them unawares. We were able to get within a few yards of the girl and her companion while they were still firing at our chaps on the hill. We then opened up with all we had and both were killed.

We recovered their arms and took back a large red and white silk Communist flag as a trophy.

18.

The Real Ending

Redvers Battersby – Corporal D Company

I was on the patrol for which Serjeant Chadwick got his medal. I'm sorry to say it was reported wrongly. After three bandits were killed, Serjeant Chadwick was watching our rear. I took Mush Monday and someone else round the back and shot the last two – a female school teacher from Penang and a young man.

I brought the lads down from the hill and collected the bodies. Serjeant Chadwick then came down. We checked our ammo and he was the only one with any left. I borrowed two mags for my Sten; then with two of the lads went to the Karangan tin mine and phoned Serjeant Major Fletcher at Kulim. He then came out with some ammo and the Malay Police.

When we got back to the scene of the fight, the Serjeant Major asked if the bodies had been searched. Chadwick said they had a few dollars on them and a tin of 393 penicillin tablets. (I kept these and crushed them to put on jungle-sores.) Later, the police searched the bodies and found thousands of dollars in new notes. When CSM Fletcher found out, he went mad with me, saying I'd let the police have our insurance money!

Weeks afterwards, the squatter area near the scene of the fight was still deserted and all the animals drifted away periodically. I think they had an officers' pig-shoot out there. It was reported in *The Bugle* that D Company had presented fresh pork to the Battalion, courtesy of the commies!

19.

Shades of Green

James Harper – Private D Company

In the Detention Barracks at Ipoh early in 1949, two veterans of the Battalion were undergoing sentences of sixty and ninety days. The prisoner serving the ninety days had no hosetops in his kit. However, he did have a pair of very bright, light green football socks with which he made do.

One morning on the Commandant's parade, the two KOYLI prisoners were standing side by side. When the Commandant looked them over, his attention was drawn to the two different shades of green of their hosetops and he demanded the reason. Quick as a flash, the prisoner serving sixty days explained that he was from the 1st Battalion KOYLI who wore dark green and the other prisoner was from the 2nd Battalion KOYLI who wore light green.

The Commandant accepted this answer and continued with his inspection.

20.

The Serjeant Major's Holiday

Redvers Battersby – Corporal D Company

Early in 1949 we had to relieve a section of Gurkhas who were laying in ambush on a track just inside the Malay – Siam border. The track was supposed to be the commies' main route across the border, so the operation was planned for fourteen days. Anyway, as we were getting ready to go, Serjeant Major Jim Fletcher came up to me and said: "Can I go with you?"

I was gob-smacked! Anyone who hasn't met Jim has never lived.

7. In bamboo jungle on the Siamese border in 1949.

Mad as a hatter, he was, but a soldier to the lads and no frills. "Why?" I asked.

"I'm fed up with just being around HQ," he said. "I want a change of scenery."

"OK, if that's what you want," I said, assuming he would take charge. "What are we taking then?"

"We've got to take all our own drinking-water," he said, "because the Gurkhas at the ambush site put a grenade in the pool to kill the fish and polluted it. But otherwise, take nothing. It's a waste of time taking washing and shaving tackle. Be like the Chindits and rough it. Anyway, I'm only coming as a rider. It's your patrol."

We got to the ambush site and set the Bren on the Siam side of the track and Sten guns along our side, and soon settled in. We were in the middle of a bamboo thicket. Regularly during the day and night, the bamboo would explode like grenades going off and shake us up. Apart from that, it was a pretty boring fortnight.

Periodically, Jim Fletcher would come up to my bivvy pissed to the wide. He stank of samsu (rice whisky). Where he got it from I don't know. All he could say was that he was enjoying his holiday and meant to do it more often. He mucked in with the lads – his CSM's insignia was in his pack – and he and the lads were on good terms. No bull at all.

The night before we were due to leave, the bamboo around the ambush site was banging like mad and monkeys and other animals were running about all over the place. It became so bad we were stood-to all night. Anyway, things quietened down and the time to leave came around. Off we went down the track to pick up our transport back.

Two hundred yards down the track, we came to a place where the bamboo had been burned. We assumed this had caused the disturbance the previous night and carried on up the side of a hill. When we got to the top and stopped for a rest, Fletcher said to me: "Look at that!"

Below us we could see for miles and found that the burned bamboo wasn't just in one place. It had been burned off all round our ambush position which stood out, a green circle, like a sore thumb. Who had done it was anybody's guess, but Fletch summed it up by saying: "Everybody but us knew we were guarding the Sultan's bamboo!"

Before we reached the road, we passed through a Malay village. When the Malays saw us, they didn't know what to do. All the kids were screaming, as we looked a terrible sight. Well, you can guess what we looked like after a fortnight without a wash, shave or change of clothes and with our clothing all ripped and stained with anti-mossy oil. When we managed to assure the Malays that we were OK, we found out that the kids had never seen a white man before. It was such a remote area that they didn't even know about the Jap occupation of Malaya or the war that had finished it.

Anyway, the Serjeant Major thought he'd had a great holiday!

21.

Animals

Jock Scurr – Private Signal Platoon

During my adolescent pre-army days, I'd always enjoyed jungle adventure films and particularly liked *Beyond the Blue Horizon* in which Dorothy Lamour was chased through the Malayan jungle by Mobok, the mad elephant. Narrow escapes from a panther and a crocodile were also featured; and there was a magnificent tiger regularly leaping around but he was a friend of Dorothy's, as a treacherous native porter discovered to his cost. Consequently, when I first went out into the real-life Malayan jungle, not only did I expect to find a Communist bandit lurking behind every bush but I also considered that I would be in grave danger of being mauled by tigers and trampled by elephants.

In the event, during forty-two operations, the only animals I ever saw in the jungle or its environs were water buffaloes, wild pigs, monkeys, snakes and lizards. Although I occasionally heard the roars of both tigers and elephants and from time to time spotted the padded-paw tracks of the former along river banks, I never once saw a tiger or an elephant and I can honestly say that this was a disappointment rather than a relief. Most of the other lads in the Battalion had much the same experience, but there were exceptions to this rule.

In the Kroh area near the Siamese border late in 1948, a patrol of C Company, commanded by Lieutenant Haddon, was proceeding through the jungle when the scouts spotted a very large elephant ahead of them. The huge beast faded out of sight into the greenery and then suddenly reappeared a few minutes later. At this point, Lieutenant Haddon came round a bend in the track to find Private Morris taking aim at the elephant's enormous rump. The officer quickly urged Morris not to fire, whereupon the elephant lumbered around to gaze with suspicion and hostility at the patrol. Without hesitation the entire patrol turned and hastily scrambled up an adjacent bank which under normal circumstances would have been considered too steep to climb!

When the elephant had departed and it was considered safe to continue up the track, the patrol shortly encountered four water buffaloes which instantly charged and once more sent the patrol into a desperate flight.

Other companies had similar experiences. For example, it is interesting to note that after Private Lyons killed B Company's first bandit at Papan in September 1948, the returning patrol had almost reached the road when they were confronted by a large wild pig that broke forth from the undergrowth. The patrol opened fire, which caused some nearby Malay Special Constables to suppose the patrol to be bandits attacking the planter's house that they were guarding. The SCs consequently began firing as well, but fortunately the pig was the only resulting casualty.

Two years after this incident, Captain Styles of B Company was awoken in his bivvy one dark night to hear a strange whirring sound passing very close outside. His Dyak tracker whispered to him that this sound indicated a swarm of mosquitoes following a tiger. Sure enough, the following morning they found the tiger's tracks just eight feet from their bivvy.

On another occasion late in 1950, Captain Styles was leading a patrol in the Klian Intan area when they came upon a water buffalo wallowing in a waterhole. After scenting them, the buffalo rose up, circled through the undergrowth, then suddenly charged straight at them. Swerving towards Private Eckley, the buffalo hit him with the side of one horn and knocked him to the ground. The buffalo now turned and charged again as Eckley stood up, and this time the beast caught the hapless

8. Elephants employed to carry supplies for C Company on an operation in Upper Perak in December 1949.

34

soldier fully with it's horns and tossed him in the air. At this point, Captain Styles was at last able to get a clear aim at the buffalo and shot it through the heart. Although Walter Eckley was badly bruised and shaken up, he had fortunately not sustained any serious injury.

As for more domesticated animals, many soldiers had pet dogs and cats, a few had monkeys and tortoises and there were even a couple who kept pigs and chickens! But dogs were the most favoured pets. When I was on detachment at Serdang early in 1951, one of our dogs became infected with rabies. The poor thing was consequently shot and buried in the rubber on the other side of the perimeter fence. That night, all the other dogs gathered around the grave and proceeded to dig up their sorely missed companion. Consequently, the body was then burned, and the dogs stood round the funeral pyre howling their heads off until the flames finally subsided. After that the dogs seemed to accept the situation and, as far as we could tell, ceased to mourn.

Finally, returning to elephants, I have always regretted that my period of service did not permit me to join C Company in time for Operation "Hornet" in December 1949. On a fourteen-day duffy, the Company departed from Grik into the wilds of Upper Perak, guided by Sakais and with supplies carried on the backs of elephants in the care of their Indian mahouts. One parachute drop of rations landed in the middle of the wide, deep and fast-flowing River Perak, but the boxes were nonetheless recovered by eager soldiers determined to retrieve the cigarettes and rum which were contained with the food.

The elephants also contributed some entertainment; especially when one of them tried to embrace Private Hendry with its trunk. But otherwise the huge beasts were not found to be greatly beneficial to jungle operations. When I was allocated to C Company six months later, Signals Lance Corporal Bill Downs told me: "The blokes following behind kept falling into big holes in the mud that they made with their feet. And the elephants were fucked! All they could manage to carry was about four crates of compo rations apiece, and even then we had to keep stopping to give them a rest."

Oh well, I suppose it would be expecting too much for elephants to be able to keep up with Light Infantry soldiers on the march!

22.

An Untimely Interruption

Fred Grundy – Lance Corporal HQ Company

Sometime in 1949 Corporal Henry Lennox and myself had come into Penang from Kulim and were having a night out down town. We both got really plastered and ended up in a brothel. Madam lined up half a dozen girls for us to choose from and we picked out the two we wanted. I was so pissed I didn't know if they were Chinese, Malays or what they were, but they were the best of a pretty awful bunch.

We each paid Madam five dollars and then went upstairs with the girls. They took us into a room that had two beds with a partition between them and there was a wardrobe opposite. Hardly had we gone into the room when we heard a jeep pulling up outside. So we rushed over to the window and looked out. As we feared, we saw that it was two MPs arriving.

"What are we going to do?" I asked my mate.

"Quick!" Henry answered. "In the wardrobe!"

We both climbed into the wardrobe and closed the door behind us. Then, as we huddled there in the darkness, we heard the MPs' boots stamping up the stairs and into the room. The wardrobe door was then wrenched open.

"OK," an MP bellowed. "Come out of there, you two bastards!"

We sheepishly climbed out, and the two MPs escorted us down the stairs and out into the street.

"Righto, lads," one of them now said calmly. "Get back to your barracks."

The MPs were generally pretty good that way. Provided you hadn't caused any trouble and weren't stupid enough to give them any lip, they didn't give you a hard time.

As we staggered up the street, I felt greatly relieved that the MPs had let us off, but Henry and I were both mad that even though we hadn't had time to do anything, we didn't get our money back!

23.

Monkey Business

Redvers Battersby – Corporal D Company

Whilst crossing the Bongsu in mid 1949, we cut a track through thick jungle from the Karangan tin mines to Terap on the other side, averaging one mile a day. A troupe of monkeys began following us and it was like a circus with them chattering above us all the time. Every morning when we left our bivouac area to continue our patrol, they would scavenge the area for bits of food; then follow us again, their noise letting everybody know we were coming. They had a leader who would watch us all the time and summon the rest of them.

On the third day, everyone was fed up with the slow progress, not knowing what was in front of us, being stung by bees, bitten by red ants and covered in leeches, but most of all fed up with the pesky monkeys. As we were settling in for the night in our next bivouac area, my leading scout, Private Abernathy, an ex-Chindit and very good  jungle fighter, came to my bivvy and said: "Corporal, I can get rid of those monkeys."

"How?" I asked.

Abernathy answered: "I'll shoot that big sod that's leading them and the rest will clear off."

"It's worth a try," I responded.

He crept out, aimed up into the trees and fired. Down came the big monkey, stone dead; and with a load of screeching all the rest bolted. Very happy with this, we had our meal and last smoke, stood-to and then bivvied down.

As usual in the jungle, we had bivvied in a circle; three men to a bivvy, one groundsheet to make a tent, one to lie on and one to cover. The sentry did an allocated time, then passed the watch on to the next man. Nobody moved out of the circle at all. Each sentry stayed still and listened and when everybody had done his time, the watch would be back with the NCO.

Anyway, all was quiet till about 2 am. Then it sounded as though it

37

was raining, so I just turned over and went back to sleep. When I was awoken again by being handed the watch, it was dawn. So I stood the men to. This consisted of lying in our bivvies facing outwards for ten minutes until it got light. But all of this time we were aware of a terrible stink.

When "Stand down!" was shouted and the men got out of their bivvies, all you could hear was men groaning and being sick and swearing: "You dirty bastards!" Our bivvies and camp site were completely covered in monkey shit. The monkeys had come back in the night and left us a present – what I'd thought was rain!

It took us five minutes to break camp and four hours to get clean when we reached a river. That was the last monkey shot by my Platoon. Monkey shit can give cat muck a hundred yards start in smell!

24.

Which Way From Here?

James Harper – Private D Company

We were in dense jungle in an extremely hilly area near Lubok Segintah in 1949. The patrol was just roaming at will, as our officer simply had no idea of direction. So it was up one side of each steep hill and down the other. After reaching the top of the third hill, the patrol was totally exhausted – so much so that a blind man could have shot us all without fear of retaliation.

The jungle was silent and the patrol was having a well-earned rest, while the officer in charge was still completely lost. Looking up at the many tall trees that were all around, the officer now detailed one of the patrol to climb one of the trees in order to view the surrounding terrain for any identifiable landmarks. After what seemed to be ages, the climber reached a considerable height and gazed around at the dense, green canopy which stretched apparently endlessly in every direction.

The officer, standing at the foot of the tree, looked up and shouted to the soldier: "Can you see anything?"

"Yes, sir," came the reply. "The white cliffs of Dover!"

25.

Swanning in a Sunderland

John Barnes – Sergeant Education Staff RAEC

Sometime in 1949, possibly shortly after the Communists had achieved total victory in China and affairs in the Far East seemed rather uncertain, the RAF Sunderland flying boats, based in Hong Kong, were sent over to Penang for some training. The training period extended over a few weeks with the planes coming over three at a time, I think, and with the crews being accommodated and fed in the Officers' or Serjeants' Mess according to rank.

As always, the Battalion took its role as host seriously and some good times were had by all. Whilst most large aircraft crews were skippered by an officer pilot, one of our visiting Sunderland crews was made up entirely of RAF warrant officers and sergeants. After one particularly convivial evening in the Serjeants' Mess with empty Tiger bottles fairly prolific, it was casually suggested that some of us "brown jobs" might care for a trip on a training flight. Whether this was contrary to RAF regulations I cannot recall.

However, a few days later, three or four of us, having gently declined our usual greasy breakfast fry-up, found ourselves aboard a flying boat racing over a fairly smooth surface in Penang harbour, and up and away we went. There were not too many flying opportunities in those days and it was all quite exhilarating. Very quickly one understood the loyalty of their crews to those wonderfully reliable Sunderlands. This one chugged happily over the sea like a somewhat shabby, run down, double-decker bus. We flew more or less due north of Penang and after half an hour or so, poor old Serjeant Stan Haley (Signals Serjeant) was slumped in a corner with a glorious green countenance – much brighter than his jungle-greens! Any rendering by Stan of "Sweet Lorraine" was obviously out of the question.

Eventually we arrived at and circled round the training area, with a small uninhabited island below us and an RAF control launch about a mile offshore. The first party trick was for the plane to descend to just above the water, zoom along and lob out depth charges. After a few runs up and down, the crew tried something a bit more exciting.

Let me set the scene. On the island beach, some RAF types had set up a fairly large target to enable the air-gunners to practise their skills. They had then taken cover in a dugout some short distance inland from the beach. At a given signal from the launch, we dived down and the front-gunner opened up full blast at the island target; the task being repeated a few times to give him some good practice. Then whilst we circled round after each run-through, the guys in the dugout would dash out to record any hits before renewing the target and then diving for cover again. In effect, the operation was controlled by radio from the launch out at sea, so it was a safe process. Well . . . almost safe!

Each air-gunner had to have his turn of course, so we went through the procedure again and again; for the rear-gunner, the starboard beam-gunner and the port beam-gunner. Whilst we couldn't get near the front and rear-gunners, a couple of us, Serjeant "Crash" Crowson (MT Platoon) and myself, were enjoying ourselves standing in the fuselage with the beam-gunners blasting away in turn.

Suddenly, a radio call came from the RAF launch to cease firing and return to Penang. Apparently we'd been too realistic – we'd shot one of the target inspectors down on the island! Our flying crew mates were pretty subdued about the affair; the skipper was probably anxious about explaining away the presence of "brown job" joyriders! Fortunately, as we later discovered, there was no fatality; the bullet had only gone through the guy's leg. Mind you, they were rather powerful bullets!

As with all unusual occurrences in the Services, a Court of Inquiry was quickly convened (at Butterworth, I think) and the unauthorised passengers required to attend. Thousands of rounds must have been fired from the Sunderland that day but every effort went into trying to discover which air-gunner had scored a hit! It's all a bit hazy now, but I think the casualty maintained that he was in the dugout at all the times he should have been, so there was a suggestion of a ricochet. But whether he was too slow off the mark or whether one of our gunner friends was too quick off the mark, I cannot recall. In fact, I don't know the outcome of the Court's findings – but why spoil a good story!

Obviously the Court of Inquiry delayed the crew's return to Hong Kong, so we had plenty of occasions to mull over the affair. The final farewell party was rather good too. I'm pretty sure I wasn't too close to the beam guns during the practice. Or was I?

26.

A Quiet Drink

Redvers Battersby – Corporal D Company

As 1949 dragged on, we were stationed at Klian Intan on the Siamese border, billeted in a school house on top of the hill overlooking the village. Our function was to send patrols up to and along the border which was boring to say the least; especially as we were always confined to camp during off-duty hours.

One night after dinner, we were fed up playing cards, so my pal Jack Smeaton said to me: "Let's sneak into the village for a drink."

"OK," I agreed, "but find out who's on guard and let him know so as he won't shoot us."

This he did and off we went down the back of the hill. I've got to admit Jacky had done this a few times before. He knew the way blindfolded and even knew the cafe owner in the village who greeted him like an old friend. As we entered the cafe, we were also welcomed by a planter we had met before. He was having a night out and was seated at a table with an attractive Chinese girl.

"Have a drink, lads," the planter said.

"OK," Jack answered, "but we'll have it in the back so nobody can see us. If we're caught down here, we'll be for it."

"That's all right," said the planter, "I'm stopping in here with this bibby."

He ordered us up two Tigers and we went through to the back room. We sat at a table and had only drunk half of our beers when all hell was let loose. The place was like a shooting gallery for about thirty seconds; then all went quiet. We jumped up and went back into the main room. It was full of gunsmoke and the planter was lying on his back on the floor, badly shot up and very dead. His weapon was gone and so was everybody.

We dived out of the door and ran back up the hill, just managing to get back to camp as the alarm sounded. So we grabbed our weapons and fell in with the rest of the Platoon. Then we all made our way down to the village and went into the cafe with the local police. Evidently the commies had been out to get the planter but hadn't known Jack and I were in the back.

When things had settled down and we were back in our billet, Jacky said to me: "Did you notice anything about that planter?"

"No," I replied.

"Well," he said, "he had a cig in his mouth but it wasn't lit. Poor bugger! They didn't even give him time to light it."

My response was to assure him that if he was planning any future nightly roaming, he'd be on his own.

27.

The Blue Plate Special

"Hutch" Hutchinson – Lance Corporal Bugle Platoon

In the second half of 1949 Tac HQ left Penang to take up residence at Batu Gajah. The camp there was built around a large empty house elevated on stilts. Pitched behind the house were a number of squad tents, and behind the right-hand line of tents stood a long row of single-storey outbuildings used as stores. One was a washroom.

Tac HQ comprised of the Bugle Platoon in its role of Defence Platoon armed with 3-inch mortars and flame-throwers, a fair number of signallers and drivers and some medical orderlies and batmen. In command was Captain Saltonstall, the Signals Officer, aided by Bugle Major Harbisher, MM.

We had just got our accommodation sorted out when we were told to attend a meeting. The purpose of the meeting was to float ideas that might make things a bit better all round for the other ranks. The best idea we ended up with suggested that all the ORs would donate one dollar each to buy potatoes, eggs, sausage and ghee (Chinese cooking fat). A kitchen of sorts would be set up in one of the empty rooms equipped with petrol cookers and all the utensils which would be needed. For the donated dollar, everyone would receive a good helping

9. Lance Corporal Hutchinson (right) and Private Smith of the Bugle Platoon at Batu Gajah in 1949, peeling potatoes for the "Blue Plate Special" – a favoured dish in diners featured in American films of the 1940s.

of sausage, egg and chips on the first night the kitchen operated. After that, the same menu would be available every night in whatever form was ordered – two eggs and chips, sausage and chips or just chips – all at reasonable prices.

Next morning, Captain Saltonstall left camp with a fistful of dollars and returned with a lorryful of rations. The Bugle Platoon provided the cook and potwashers, and we opened for business that night before the sausage could go off. The plates of lovely grub were handed out to all the dollar-donators and we did not receive one complaint.

From then on, the "Blue Plate Specials" were in great demand, providing a healthy cash flow into Tac HQ funds which bought those little extras; and they were also a good morale booster. A tropical moon, good company, a large plate of sausage, egg and chips, followed by a large bottle of cold Tiger beer – what more could you wish for?

28.

Yield to None!

Jock Scurr – Private Signal Platoon

Included among the many stories of personal experience told in this book are accounts of some of the dramatic events that are well known to KOYLI Malaya veterans. But there were other celebrated incidents about which, regrettably, no first-hand accounts have reached me. I am thinking particularly of four occasions.

When Private O'Reilly of D Company won his DCM in January 1949. Seeing a bandit about to hurl a grenade at Second Lieutenant Wigg and a Bren-gunner, O'Reilly brought the man down with a flying leap and rolled down the hillside struggling with him. The grenade rolled after them and exploded, wounding O'Reilly in the face and side. But the plucky little Private held on to his man until Mr Wigg and the Bren-gunner reached them and quickly shot the bandit dead.

When two small B Company vehicles were ambushed on the Kroh-Klian Intan road in December 1949. As the bandit gang finished off his four comrades who were lying on the road beside him, the badly wounded Private "Ginger" Fry did not flinch as a bullet just missed his head. Continuing to play dead, he felt hands removing the bandolier of ammunition from around his waist. Fry remained motionless and thereby escaped with his life, as did Major Sutcliffe who had managed to conceal himself in the belukar nearby.

And when Lance Corporal Hall of D Company won the BEM while playing billiards in the Georgetown NAAFI in May 1950. A terrorist had slung a grenade through the window, landing it on the billiard table. While others dived to the floor, Hall picked up the grenade and threw it back out again.

To end on a lighter note, I was amazed when I heard a story about Corporal Tom Morgan. When he was due to go on leave from A Company's base at Kroh, one time, he was chagrined to discover that transport and escort were not available. Determined not to lose a single day of his leave, Tom set out alone and journeyed down the extremely dangerous Baling road, seated in the back of a ramshackle civilian bus with a Bren gun held at the ready across his knees. What a nutter!

All of these men clearly lived up to the KOYLI regimental motto: *Cede Nullis* – Yield to None!

29.

Dope Smugglers

Raymond Bays – Private C Company

I was in 9 Platoon, C Company at the time of a particular incident which took place during 1949. Our Platoon Commander, Lieutenant Haddon, was very firm but also fair. I was also under Serjeant Bell and Corporal Mould, both very good mates. I may add that's how all the lads in C Company treated our NCOs. When Lieutenant Haddon wasn't in earshot, we called our NCOs by their first names and a strong sense of loyalty and comradeship was maintained. Everyone was on the best of terms.

One morning in July 1949, 8 and 9 Platoons were ordered to go to a place on the way to the Siamese border called Alor Star. Headquarters was on an old Japanese airfield with a main road running past it. Our billet was just a few yards from the road and locals used to ride and walk by. Some of their bikes used to be laden with goods going I knew not where, as we were not allowed into the town.

It was from here that 8 Platoon was ordered, on information received from the Malay Police, to lay an ambush across the border, just on the Malay side. Word had it that smugglers bringing raw narcotics into Malaya were being led by bandits; how many was not disclosed to us. However, the ambush was duly laid. The commander of 8 platoon was Second Lieutenant Thorne and I think the Serjeant was Hutchinson; we called him Hutchy.

Anyway, we were later told what happened on the night of the ambush. A party of smugglers came along the track led by, as it turned out, one solitary bandit armed with what we were told was a Thompson sub-machine-gun. The members of the party were nearly all within range of the ambushers when Mr Thorne opened fire with his Sten on

45

the leader, bringing him down. After that, panic and chaos took over as the smugglers dropped everything they were carrying and bolted back over the border.

Meanwhile, the Platoon lay and waited till dawn in case anyone came back, but no one did. So Mr Thorne decided to head back to camp with the dead bandit trussed to a bamboo pole. When the Platoon arrived back, the body was dumped on the roadside on orders from the police, so that the local people could see it as they passed by. At the same time, the Malay Police took charge of the bandit's sub-machine-gun.

That same morning, 9 Platoon, including myself , was ordered back to the same place to lay a further ambush, because it was thought that someone would come back to recover what had been dropped. But after a very sticky night, nothing had happened, so Mr Haddon ordered us to make a thorough search of a wide area. We found quite a lot of fairly large parcels which contained raw opium and, according to the police officer who was with us, a Malay by the name of Leon, another drug named chandu. All in all, he reckoned the haul was worth about

10. 9 Platoon, C Company in 1949. Raymond Bays is fifth from left, middle row, and Corporal Mould sixth with Serjeant "Taggy" Bell in front of him. First on left, front row, is Charlie McAllister, later to serve in 8 Platoon.

500,000 Malayan dollars. This, we thought, was quite a feather in our caps because it denied the bandits a substantial sum of money that they needed to run their operations.

For the next week, further ambushes were laid but nothing happened, so we were piled onto 3-tonners and taken back to Ipoh.

30.

Ghosts and Remembrance

George Williams – Private B Company

One night in Glugor Barracks, Penang, I did a stag at the magazine compound. I was marched down to the magazine which was enclosed by a fifteen to twenty-foot chain link fence. The Guard Commander unlocked the gate so that I could relieve the previous sentry, a lad called Kinchin or Kitchen. It was two o'clock in the morning. I started to walk round the perimeter of the half-blown-up magazines. About half-way through my period of stag, I heard the sound of marching men. Thinking little of it, I walked round again. Then, right opposite the magazine which had been blown up, I heard the marching sound all around me. The hair on my neck stood up. Although I couldn't see anyone, I was very glad my stag would soon be over.

I queried these sounds the next day. At the other end of the magazines there was a rifle range, but I was assured that no one had been near the range, as indeed I would expect at that time of the night. Then, some old soldier who had been to Penang before, during the war, said that a platoon of Japs had been killed in an ambush at the magazine by some Aussies. Consequently, the place was reputed to be haunted. No wonder no one liked doing the magazine guard!

These ghostly marching men put me in mind of when B Company was stationed at Tapah late in 1949. We were on what had once been a rubber plantation. The Japs had cut down all the trees, leaving just the stumps sticking up all over the place. At this time we had the Coldstream Guards beside us and when they were on stag, they used to shoot at nothing all through the night. Well, we all knew what it was like. If you looked at the tree stumps in the darkness, they would almost form up in threes and march away!

One day at Tapah, I was sitting on my charpoy cleaning my Bren mags, having deposited my ammo rounds into my helmet on the floor between my feet. All of a sudden – bang! – one of the other lads had loosed off a round which shot right between my legs and through the side of my helmet, knackering a few of my rounds before it came out the other side. It was what you would call a very narrow squeak.

Another day, we were on a patrol and halted for a rest. Major De Butts and two serjeants went off into the jungle. After a short while, they came running back along the track. One of them had stepped on a hornets' nest. We could hardly recognise them. They were covered in large lumps all over their bodies and were in terrible pain. The MI orderly treated them as best he could.

Although only as big as houseflies, hornets were really fierce when disturbed. As for leeches, they could even get through the eyelets of our canvas boots and there was nowhere on the human body they couldn't reach. I took to wearing a "johnny" on patrol to stop the leeches getting to my private parts. Through constant sweating and regular downpours of rain, we were never dry in the jungle and were also persistently afflicted by foot-rot, tinea, ringworm and prickly heat. These were everyday ailments, additional to the more serious risks of malaria and scrub typhus.

I can also recall a patrol near Tapah when my pal Marsh and myself were in the last section. As we came over a hill, I suddenly spotted a bandit camp and a bandit sighting us up with his Bren. My feet slipped from under me and my Sten gun jammed as the Bren opened fire. Marsh and I had a lucky escape but our Sakai guide was shot. Strangely, he ran about 200 yards, dead on his feet. The bandits had gone, however, before we could get any of them.

One night on another patrol, we were bivvied down in the ulu (jungle). Early in the morning, our medical orderly, a chap called Kilbride, had a nightmare and came running down the track shouting wildly. Some of the lads started shooting but luckily they missed him. I think that cured Kilbride of his nightmare!

I always remember the hard times – and some good ones – that we had out East and I especially remember the lads who didn't come back, who – as the famous remembrance quotation says – "shall grow not old as we that are left grow old. . ."

After I came home from Malaya, for more than eighteen months I couldn't stand having people behind me; I used to cross over to the other side of the road. And I once travelled to Birmingham by train and found myself picking out all the likely ambush spots along the route.

Although most of the men in the 2nd/1st KOYLI were conscripts, they were a great bunch of lads and I feel proud to have served with every one of them. If I could live my life again, I would like to have these same lads around me once more.

31.

Far From Humdrum

Redvers Battersby – Corporal D Company

Not all patrols were humdrum. I recall a few that weren't. Patrolling up on the border and pinching the border-stone to save us from being interned in Siam.

Crossing a knee-deep river in the Baling area and feeling hard bumps on our legs. These turned out to be caused by turtles. We stopped there for a rest and bath. Soldiers were going up and down stream like the clappers on the turtles' backs. And one was taken back to camp for turtle soup.

Discovering the lovely hot water ponds at Ayer Panas and soldiers wading fully clothed into the hot water, washing their clothes and having a bath at the same time.

When on patrols in the Klian Intan and Kaki Bukit areas, it was not uncommon to find a tribe of Sakais tagged on to the back of the patrol in the middle of nowhere. We used to bring them back to Klian Intan Police Station, as the police were required to feed them and keep them until they decided to go back into the jungle.

The Sakais used to come and watch our football matches. They were in bands of about thirty. Not one of them was taller than four feet and every one of them used to smoke. At our matches, it was comical to see all the men and women puffing away. We got used to them, so we let them have one side of the field to themselves. When the ball was kicked off, the headman would race up the touchline, following the ball up and down the field, with all the tribe behind him shouting away. It reminded us of school being let out.

But the Sakais always disappeared as quickly as they appeared and the first and last thing they scrounged was a fag.

32.

Soap and Suspense

Bill Lyness – Private B Company

On 2 November 1949, 5 Platoon, B Company set off for a three-day jungle patrol in the Kulim area. We marched throughout the first day and made camp at about 5 pm.

At 8 am the next day, we set out again and marched for two hours. We then stopped for a rest on a jungle ridge overlooking a valley that was covered in mist. After about ten minutes, Major Sutcliffe and Lance Corporal O'Brien went off on a scouting mission. They came back some time later with the good news that they had found evidence of a bandit camp in the valley below. This evidence was a bar of soap by the edge of a pond.

When we had made our way down into the valley, Major Sutcliffe issued his orders to prepare for action. Corporal Pudwell, Private Brown and myself with my Bren gun would be placed at the edge of the trees overlooking the pond. On the other side of the pond, the bar of soap lay beside a track which led up through the undergrowth to dense trees where the bandit camp was possibly situated. The rest of the Platoon would proceed round to the right of the pond and take the bandit camp from the rear. This would then push the bandits into our line of fire. A good plan that we all hoped would work.

At this stage of the operation, there was a thick mist covering the pond and the opposite hillside. This gave the rest of the Platoon cover so that they could creep up on the bandit camp unseen. It was quite a bit of luck on our part, because within twenty minutes or so, the mist

50

11. Private Bill Lyness of B Company on a more relaxing occasion, swimming in the pool at Glugor Barracks in 1949.

started to rise and Pudwell, Brown and I could now clearly see the pond and the wooded hillside beyond.

The first indication that the plan might be a success was when two uniformed bandits came down the hill to the pond, both carrying rifles. They put their rifles down and both had a good wash in the pond. At this stage, we knew we could not fire until the rest of the Platoon had got into position. After a couple of minutes, the two bandits finished washing, picked up their rifles and went back up the hill.

We now knew the Major had been right about the bandit camp and that we would be in action very shortly. The suspense was something I shall never forget and it lasted for quite a long time. The excitement must have been too much for Corporal Pudwell, because he just dropped his pants and couldn't hold his motion. The smell and excitement were hell! The things that went through my mind were: had we done the right thing to let the two bandits go back to the camp? Should we have shot them? After all, they were only 200 yards away and easy pickings for a Bren gun.

It was then that the firing started and all hell broke out. Two bandits

51

ran down the hill opposite, then turned right along a track with two 5 Platoon lads in hot pursuit, firing as they ran. Brown and I then opened fire and the two bandits fell to the ground. Pudwell still had his pants down and was unable to do anything. It's debatable who shot the bandits but the result was two bandits less. After the firing stopped at the camp, the final tally was four dead bandits and two women bandits captured. So I was reassured that things had turned out right in the end and that my two companions and I had done the correct thing earlier.

We stayed the rest of the day and all night in the bandit camp, enjoying the luxury of bamboo beds and excellent washing facilities. One more bandit came back to the camp in the night and was shot by the sentry. We found him the next day. We took the two women back with us and handed them over to the police. Some time later, they were both sentenced to five years in prison.

One thing that made us all laugh was when Private Titmarsh, the medical orderly, was asked what part he had played in the action. In reply, he described how he had sprayed the jungle with bullets. But when he was afterwards asked how many rounds he needed to replenish his bandolier, he answered: "Three rounds, please!"

33.

The Devil in a Brandy Bottle

Roy Caldecott – Lance Corporal A Company

As 1949 neared its end, I had for some time become quite friendly with a little lady called Maureen Lessler. Maureen was Eurasian, born of a Dutch father and Philippine mother. She it was who served me with my brandy and dry ginger at the bar of the Piccadilly dance hall in Georgetown, and due to whom I had already earned myself two severe reprimands from our CO. On occasional trips to Penang during my first fifteen months or so in Malaya, the nights "down town" had been getting more like a routine. First, a mate and myself would have a meal in the Boston or Broadway; then a short trishaw ride to the City Lights where we would hand over our dance tickets and any spare dollars to the hostesses who caught our eye.

For some weeks, I had forsaken this routine and headed straight for the Piccadilly. It was much better than having my eardrums damaged by some Chinese soprano trying to "Begin the Beguine". Maureen couldn't understand why I chose to sit at the bar, drink my brandy and just talk while waiting for her to finish work at midnight. We would then share a trishaw to her aunt's house where Maureen lived with her older sister Hazel; each time knowing that auntie's house was "Out of Bounds" and when Maureen finished work I was AWOL (absent without leave). It didn't, at the time, worry a boy of just 20 what terrors lurked in the dark alleyways of foreign lands. This boy had a lady at his side and the world was his.

One night on leaving the Piccadilly, we directed ourselves to our regular seat in a trishaw, Maureen gave the man instructions in her usual tongue, and I found we were taking a different road.

"I hope you like our new hotel," Maureen said.

"What was wrong with your aunt's place?" I asked.

"I don't like Hazel's ideas," was her reply.

So off we sped towards the bus station. I thought – I hope she doesn't think I'm going back to camp just yet! The trishaw stopped. Out leapt Maureen, dragging me by the arm after her. A door opened and in we went. An ancient Chinese man, smoking his pipe, sat at a small table at the foot of the stairs.

"Do you want supper?" Maureen asked me.

"Whatever you order will do for me, " I answered and added: "Can we get something to drink?"

"Sure."

The old man followed us up the stairs, carrying a tray with two bowls. We sat and ate our supper. Maybe a few minutes later, we heard a tap-tap on the door. Maureen opened the door and in stepped Hazel, carrying another tray with a pot of coffee and a double brandy on it. The brandy was set on the table in front of me.

"Yours, " said Maureen.

"Ours," said Hazel, setting down the coffee pot and going to a sideboard for two cups.

The three of us sat round the table and while they talked in their mother tongue, I sipped my brandy. The drinks finished, Hazel disappeared with seven dollars which the old man had asked her to get for room and supper, and I added two dollars for the drinks.

Maureen and I now retired to bed. Half-conscious and half-dozing off, I remember Maureen's right hand chasing her left hand, exploring my body with no result.

"Come!" she ordered at last. Taking me by the hand, she led me out to the verandah where I saw a large earthenware jar which was set under the eaves in order to catch rainwater.

"Stand there!" she ordered. And bowl after bowl of ice-cold water was poured over me. She then went back into the room, brought back a towel, and while I dried myself, she tidied the sheets on the bed.

When I returned, she was lying propped up on the pillows, one hand behind her head, the other outstretched towards me. No other invitation

12. Lance Corporal Roy Caldecott when based at Grik with A Company in 1949.

was needed. I joined her and we covered our naked bodies with a single sheet.

"You shouldn't make a girl work so hard for her love," she scolded me after a while.

"It must be the devil in the brandy bottle," I claimed as an excuse.

"Next time, no brandy," she said. "Next time, I give you something to make love long time. Promise me you'll take it and no questions."

"OK," I agreed, and to make my promise secure I managed it once more – just in time before the tap-tap on the door again. Maureen got up and opened the door, and in came Hazel. I looked questioningly at Maureen.

"You are in her side of the bed," she explained.

I moved into the middle, patting the warm space I had just vacated, silently inviting Hazel. In response, she slid under the sheet and accepted the embrace of my right arm around her shoulder; the left one was already claimed by Maureen who said quietly: "We sleep now." So, with two beautiful female bodies, black hair, coffee-coloured skin, dark-tipped breasts, pressed against me, I managed to sleep a little.

It was early. Dawn had broken. I looked to left and right. The girls were fast asleep. How could I get out of there without disturbing them? I pondered over the problem. There was only one way – down the centre and out at the foot of the bed. This action decided, I took hold of the sheet, raised it a little and slowly inched my way down until I could feel nothing under my heels. Not much further to go now.

When my head reached halfway, I turned very carefully over onto my stomach, then slowly moved a few more inches down. I now put my lips to Maureen's raised hip and kissed my thanks to her flesh. To my shock, I felt her hand come over and press my face into her skin. Then, on sudden impulse, I turned my head and did the same to Hazel's hip. And this time I was surprised by both of Hazel's hands pressing my head down into her body. A promise of things to come? Perhaps not, but a wonderful thought!

Once out of the bed, I got into my shirt and slacks and slipped on my shoes. As I quietly made my way out and down the stairs, I looked at my watch. It was 04.00 hours. There wasn't much time. I had to waken the old man to let me out. This he did and then shook my hand vigorously. After waking a taxi driver at the station, I journeyed back to Glugor Barracks to receive my third rep a few hours later.

On my being marched out of the CO's office, the RSM recommended I put my stripes back on with a zip!

34.

Death in the Lallang

Ted Slade – Private D Company

Private Ward was a National Serviceman. I don't recall his first name; I always called him "Wardy". His parents may have been dead as he was living with his grandmother before his call-up. He was a shy, quiet lad and I don't think he'd ever been with a woman. I sometimes used to joke with him and say: "Never mind, Wardy. The next time we're in Penang, I'll take you down town and introduce you to Dumb Mary!" I think he always took it in good heart.

On 8 November 1949 the Company set out from Kulim on a three-day operation. We made a base that night near Anak Kulim and the next day, 10 Platoon was ready to go out on patrol. Before we left, Ward suddenly turned and said to Corporal Reynolds: "When you get back to Kulim, there's ten dollars in my mess-tin. See that my grandmother gets it." Reynolds thought this was rather strange but otherwise thought no more of it at the time.

As I recall, there were twenty-four of us who set out on that patrol. In command was Second Lieutenant Richards and the Platoon Serjeant was called Holmes. At about 4.45 pm, we were marching in file up a hill of lallang (elephant grass) which had a few isolated rubber trees dotted here and there. On the summit of the hill, a wooden basha stood upon a flat earth mound. As the scouts neared the top, we suddenly came under a heavy fire from the mound.

Just beside me was a pile of logs which I promptly dived behind. Then I heard a voice to my rear calling: "Help me! Help me!" It was Ward. I crawled back and found him lying beside a rubber tree with a bullet-wound in his chest. I pulled his shirt open and reached for my field-dressing. Remembering what I'd been told in training, I picked up a small stone and started to place it inside the dressing; I think the idea was to prevent air from getting into the hole in the chest.

56

At that moment, however, bullets began ricocheting off the rubber tree just above my head. They were being fired by a bandit positioned on a track over to my left. He obviously had me in his sights. I made a split-second, live-or-die decision and was back behind my pile of logs in no time. It was a case of self-preservation, but I knew from the look of that bloody hole in his chest that Wardy was probably a goner anyway and there was nothing to be gained by having two men dead instead of one.

Immediately to my right lay another National Service lad. He had messed himself and the smell was really awful. Beyond him was Serjeant Holmes who yelled over to me, asking if I had any grenades. So I threw a grenade over to him. (It was later reported that Serjeant Holmes crawled to within fifteen yards of the bandits and threw six grenades among them, preventing them from enveloping the patrol's flank.)

It was estimated that there were more than sixty bandits opposing us, and they certainly had a good supply of ammunition as they kept up a continuous fire against us for two and three-quarter hours. My field of fire was very restricted as the patrol was dispersed up the hill to my front and right. I didn't want to waste my ammo but loosed off eight or nine rounds in the direction of the firing coming from my left. Most of the action was up at the front, beneath the basha on the earth mound where Second Lieutenant Richards was organising things pretty coolly, it was said. I couldn't see what was happening up there and only remember hearing that the Bren-gunner narrowly dodged a grenade that was slung at him. All the while, I regularly heard Ward calling out: "Mother! Mother!" It was really heart-rending.

When darkness fell around 7.30 pm, the bandits suddenly ceased fire. It was then that someone up front shouted out: "What's the matter, Johnny? Have you gone for a NAAFI-break?"

After a short period of continuous silence, Second Lieutenant Richards and a couple of others crept forward and verified that the bandits had gone. The rest of us were then called up the hill and into the basha where we were organised in all-round defence positions. Second Lieutenant Richards went back down the hill and when he came back, he said: "Slade's dead."

"What?" I exclaimed, hearing my name.

"Sorry!" he corrected himself. "I mean Ward."

Many times since, I have wondered if I might have somehow been able to save Wardy. But in that situation, with a severe chest-wound and no medical aid available, I'm as sure as I can be that there wasn't really anything anyone could have done to prevent the inevitable.

We were very fearful that the bandits would hit us again during the night. Some of the lads were down to ten rounds, so the Lieutenant gathered in all the ammunition and redistributed it amongst us equally. We remained on fifty per cent stand-to throughout the night, but the enemy did not return.

Next morning, we set off down the track that had been to my left during the battle, carrying Ward's body and the body of a bandit who had been killed at the top of the hill. We also picked up another dead one on the track, opposite where Ward and I had come under fire. When we reached a track junction a little further down, we came upon another body but by this time we had quite enough to carry in relays, so we left it, just as we left another two or three bodies that were

13. Men of 10 Platoon, D Company in 1949. Private Ken Ward is centre, front row, and Corporal Donald Reynolds is on right, back row.

scattered about the hill. We made our way very cautiously in case the bandits were once more lying in ambush and for once there was no shortage of volunteers to take a turn at carrying the Bren!

However, we reached the Company base safe and unmolested. A follow-up patrol was sent out which located a camp near the hill, from which the bandits had fled. It was big enough to accommodate 100.

Second Lieutenant Richards and Serjeant Holmes were awarded the MC and MM respectively for their parts in the action. The rest of us awarded ourselves as much Tiger as we could drink!

35.

Dinner at the Broadway

Roy Caldecott – Lance Corporal A Company

Ever since my early teenage days, I had been blessed with the ability to play a fair game of soccer. I loved the game and always gave 100 per cent; hard but fair, no quarter given or taken. One of my greatest memories is of when I was first chosen to play for our Battalion. At the time, it was our pleasure to entertain the crews of any of the British Navy craft that happened to be at anchor in our waters and challenge them to a match.

One such game was against a team from HMS *Amethyst*, following their adventure on the Yangtze River early in 1949. The sailors still had their sea legs and were no match for our well acclimatised and very fit team. Another was when we travelled down to Port Swettenham to play against the Gurkhas in the FARELF Cup. We lost. The little devils ran rings around us. When enjoying a large Tiger that evening in the NAAFI, I learned that they had a First Division League player training and coaching them. He was stationed close by, doing his National Service in the RAF. He had done a good job as his team was well-drilled and very efficient.

For our home games, players from the rifle companies would be called in from the mainland to play on the Saturday and return to their duties on the Sunday. These games were therefore a bonus for us, providing us with a night off in Penang. One such opportunity came as 1949 drew to a close.

After the match, I had a quick shower and caught the first bus into town. Maureen and Hazel were still living with the old man in the house near the bus station. It was about this time I learned that the old man was their great uncle who, in his younger years, had been a well-known herbalist. In the back room of the house, I had seen a collection of large bottles of alcohol preserving, I remember, lizards' tails, hens' feet, bats' tongues – the list could go on, the memory can't. And there was drawer after drawer of leaf, root, twig, flower, etc.

Getting off the bus, I could see Chan Liew – which by this time the old man insisted I call him – sitting on his chair at the open door.

"Getting a little sun and fresh air," he said in broken English. Helping myself to another chair from the hallway, I sat with him and chatted for some time.

"I wondered who Uncle Chan was talking to," said Maureen from the open door.

"I have some tailoring to collect from the Bazaar," I told her. "Can we have an early dinner before you start work?"

"Yes. Where would you like to go?"

"After I pick up my shirts, I thought we would go to the Broadway."

"OK. I'll get changed." And off she went into the shadows of the house.

"You have a surprise coming," said Chan Liew, but he wouldn't elaborate no matter how I probed him.

At last, about 6 pm, Maureen came out and stood in the sunlight between Chan and me, wearing a scarlet silk cheongsam. Wow! She looked beautiful! She also wore a white flower behind her left ear which was a silent clue to Eastern people that she was spoken for. Walking down to the Bazaar, I was sure my new shirts wouldn't fit me; my chest seeming to have grown at least three inches since she had clasped my hand in hers when leaving Chan Liew. When we reached the Bazaar and collected my two new shirts, one cream, the other pale green, she fell for the cream one, so we had her measured for a cheongsam of the same material. I paid the lady eleven dollars and it was worth every cent.

At the Broadway, the waitress was showing us to a table in the main room but I guided her to a booth which was more private. Maureen ordered a salad for herself and a steak for me.

"I thought you would be hungry after your game today," she explained. "So I have ordered a special steak for you. I hope you will manage it."

I was ravenous. "I'll manage," I promised.

"I've heard you say that somewhere before," she chided with a naughty wink.

First to arrive was a tray with a small Chinese teapot and two Chinese tea-bowls. Taking a small package out of her shoulder bag, Maureen said: "This is from Uncle Chan."

"What is it?" I asked.

"You promised not to ask any questions," she reminded me. "I'll show you."

She opened the package and I could see some shredded leaves, a few shavings of bark and three or four twigs inside. Putting this potion into the teapot, she called the waitress back and told her to fill the pot with boiling water. When the pot was returned and placed on the table, the look on the girl's face told me she knew what it was for. Smiling at Maureen and me, she left with the words: "Have a good night, sir!"

After we had emptied the pot, our meal arrived. The special steak turned out to be a T-bone, served with two jacket potatoes and three veg. When the meal was over, I released my belt a notch.

"Thank you for the special," I said.

"You deserve it," she replied, and then, "I've something else to show you."

She reached into her bag and placed upon the table a chain with a heart-shaped medallion. I spread out the chain and saw it was longer than normal. The medallion was enamelled with small stones around the outer edge. It would have looked well with what Maureen was wearing but she wouldn't allow me to put the chain around her neck.

"It is not for there," she said, leaving me puzzled. She then opened her bag and produced a matchbox.

"I didn't know you used matches," I said.

"Boxes hold other things," she replied. And sliding the box open, she shook out a dead wasp onto my near-empty plate. Then, after shouting for the waitress, she stabbed at my plate and screamed: "What do you call that?"

The girl was speechless.

"Bring the manager!" Maureen demanded irately.

Everyone in the cafe was now either standing up or making some other move in order to see into our booth. The manager promptly arrived. I couldn't look him in the face. After he and Maureen had exchanged words in a local dialect, he suddenly took hold of my hand and said: "Will you accept my apologies please, sir?"

The waitress hurriedly gathered our plates, bowls and teapot onto a tray and the pair of them left. Not many minutes later, the manager returned and pressed into my hand two green cards on which was written: "With the management's sincere apologies and regards, we extend to you and your company an invitation to dinner here next Christmas. All will be provided free of charge. We will be so happy to entertain you for the whole evening." And it was signed by the manager, whose name I can't recall.

I expressed my thanks as best I could. Maureen had amazed me – and the night was still young!

36.

Out of Bounds

Redvers Battersby – Serjeant A Company

While in Penang for Company rest, another serjeant and myself went down town for a night out. There was an elderly lady in Georgetown who I knew well from when I had been Provost Corporal. Every time I went to the City Lights, she was there pimping as she owned a brothel. She always swopped me a cigar for cigs.

This particular night, we had a few drinks and decided to end the night in the "Out of Bounds" area. So I said to Princess (as I called the old lady): "Have you owt for supper?" She answered yes; so after the City Lights closed, me and my mate set off to her house.

We were both sitting in the kitchen when I saw a serjeant major and another serjeant from our Battalion in the foyer pricing the girls with Princess. Then off up the stairs they went. A little later, still in the

14. Serjeants of A Company (left to right) "Tug" Wilson, Bill McCarthy and Redvers Battersby having a farewell drink in the home of Serjeant Fred Thomas in April 1950. Mrs Thomas also in picture.

kitchen eating, I suddenly heard the MPs shouting to Princess: "Are there any soldiers in here?"

I dashed round the back and up the stairs to the landing and shouted down: "What's up?"

An MP yelled: "Any soldiers up there?"

In my broadest Yorkshire I shouted back: "Nay, lad, there's only us American seamen!" I then scuttled back down to the kitchen.

There was silence. Then the MP exclaimed: "Americans, my arse! They're Koylis!" and raced upstairs.

I heard a window open and when we looked out of the kitchen door, we saw two naked men, with just boots on, their clothes under their arms, running for their lives up the street towards another brothel. Anyway, they got away and we stayed doggo until the MPs had gone.

Next morning at breakfast in the Serjeants' Mess, the two in question were sitting near me and my mate. So I shouted to the Mess Serjeant: "We saw a great sight last night – two bare-arsed swaddies racing to be first in the brothel!"

If looks could kill, I wouldn't be here.

37.

When the Bells Tolled

Roy Caldecott – Lance Corporal A Company

We had left A Company's base at Kulim and had been patrolling Dublin Estate for some days. It was 25 January 1950 and was our fifteenth day on this operation. Bob Raynor and I were out front, scouting. We took the lead in turn and were glad we were in rubber. The track was well used and the going was easy.

When the gunfire started, whoever was leading pushed the one following behind the large root of an Ipoh tree – what was known as "taking cover." Maybe Bob had seen the grenade drop. I hadn't. It must have landed on the other side of the root. A few seconds later, the explosion had caused a vacuum around us. I remember finding breathing a little difficult and there seemed to be a campanologist in my head.

The lads behind us were moving from tree to tree. Bob shook my shoulder and pointed back down the track to where my jungle hat had been blown. The bells in my head stopped ringing and we were soon on the move once again.

If any reader suffers from ear-wax, the above-mentioned remedy is not recommended!

38.

Tally Ho!

Redvers Battersby – Serjeant A Company

In January 1950 during a battalion operation in the Terap area, my Platoon was in the lead of A Company with Captain Rome in command. We were in an overgrown rubber plantation which was being worked. Following an uphill path, we approached a small house. My position in the file was at the back, being Platoon Serjeant. The lad in front of me was from a new intake and being "broken in", so I had given him the EY (grenade-throwing) rifle to carry.

As the patrol passed the house, two women came out onto the path and shouted up the hill in Chinese. Two minutes later, we came under fire. The head of the column stopped and we spread out in the rubber trees and worked our way up till. we were in line, with a man positioned behind every tree. All in the line were pinned down by the enemy fire. The only people who could move were myself and the lad with the EY rifle, slightly to the rear.

At that moment, Serjeant Wilson came up on my left with his Platoon. I shouted: "Tally Ho!" He replied to confirm he was a friend and then joined us.

In my own Platoon, the first man to my right was Lance Corporal Caldecott. I shouted to him: "Tell the lads to hold their fire while we outflank them!"

His reply was: "What?"

So I shouted it again but got the same reply. I now said to Tug Wilson: "Wait." After I'd dropped my equipment off, I jumped behind an adjacent rubber tree and then jumped behind Lance Corporal Caldecott's tree. I told him what I'd shouted before and added: "Give me a minute. Then pass the message."

"OK," he said.

As I jumped back away from the tree, a figure stood up and threw a grenade. When the smoke cleared, Caldecott shouted: "Did you do that?" You can imagine my answer to that, seeing as I'd lost a bit of skin off my head!

Anyway, I got back to Tug Wilson and told him what was going to happen. I then said to the EY lad: "Can you use that?"

"No," he replied. So I took the weapon from him and fired it in the direction we would be going; then told him just to use the rifle to fire 303 ammo. When the grenade exploded amongst the enemy, it did the trick and we were able to advance to the top of the hill.

Then, as we were forming up to sweep on, I saw a movement on the ground under a nearby tree. I quickly leapt on top of what turned out to be a commie trying to line up to shoot Caldecott. So I lowered my Sten barrel and blew his brains out.

Second Lieutenant Sibbald now came up and called the sweep off. We tied the body to a pole and marched away. On our way back to

Terap Police Station, we called at the house and took the two women who had raised the alarm prisoner. When we reached the road, the CO stopped his armoured car to congratulate us.

As we had stripped the women's house of everything we wanted, it was chicken dinners that night with plenty of hot, sweet coffee.

39.

Dropped Right In It

Ivor Lewis – Corporal Signal Platoon

It was customary on long duffies to carry three days' supply of food rations and then be replenished by air drop. One time in the Kulim area in January 1950, I was with B Company on a combined operation with D Company. We had received an air drop by a DC3-Dakota aircraft, carried out further patrols for three days and then prepared a clearing in the jungle for a second drop.

I was operating a "68" wireless set in order to communicate with the aircraft, giving our location and dropping information. A fluorescent panel was laid in the centre of the clearing and at the appointed time, a smoke flare was ignited to indicate position and wind direction. When the Dakota came within sight, I contacted the aircraft to give the pilot guidance for the run-in to the Dropping Zone. I must add here that the DZ was situated alongside a river and the fluorescent panel was placed some yards away from the bank.

The pilot informed me that he would make a drop on the second run-in, which he duly did. The drop was quite successful with the exception of one parachute which landed fair and square in the river. I acknowledged the drop to the pilot and somehow my microphone pressel-switch became stuck in the transmit position. The Company Commander, Major Sutcliffe, was standing beside the "68" set at the time. When he saw the parachute splash into the water, he declared: "What a bloody awful drop!"

Just after this remark, I realised that the microphone switch had stuck and I managed to release it just in time to hear the pilot respond in a

15. Corporal Ivor Lewis operating a "62" set while on an earlier patrol with D Company in 1949.

strong Australian accent: "If you can bloody-well do any better, cobber, come up and drop it your bloody self!"

This transmission was heard all around the area by all involved in the operation, including the Gurkhas. Was my face red for quite a while! And certain members of the Company reminded me of the incident for a long time afterwards.

40.

A Picnic to Remember

Roy Caldecott – Lance Corporal A Company

On Sunday 29 January 1950, A Company returned to Kulim. We had been on this little stroll since the 10th and were glad that we would once again be able to sleep with our backs on beds. The following day, several of us applied for a much-needed break, and on Tuesday 31st I found myself, along with Bob Raynor and Tug Wilson, on a 15-cwt heading for Penang on ten days' glorious leave.

We arrived at Sandycroft Leave Centre at about 10.30 am, just in time to get some sand between our toes before lunch. There was a two-person rowing boat which was already occupied by two Hussars. We didn't feel like walking along the beach. After all, we had just finished a three-week hike in Dublin Estate. So we decided to laze on the sand until the rowing boat became free. It was then we learned that a list was made for the boat day by day. Bob and I found the boy who kept the list and put our names down for Thursday at 2 pm.

Over the table at tea-time, Bob and Tug were making plans to see a film. But I was thinking it was about time I let Maureen know I was on the island. In the rest room after tea, they found a *Straits Times* and went through the list of cinemas, looking for a decent film. They settled for *The Third Man* at the Odeon, I think, or it may have been the Rex.

I was soon on a bus going into Georgetown and duly called in at Great Uncle Chan Liew's house. Once again I found him sitting outside. As I approached, he smiled. I can see that smile now. The years had been very unkind to the old man. Several gaps where there should have been teeth greeted me.

"You looking for little Maureen?" he said, shaking my hand.

"Yes. Is she inside?" I asked.

"No. Gone back to auntie's two weeks ago. Only Hazel here now."

Going to the open door, I called: "Hazel!"

"Yes. Moment please," came the reply.

I sat with the old man as I had done many times before and offered him my cigarette packet. He paused a little. Previously, I had often treated him with a corona cigar. This time I said: "Sorry, no cigar today."

He took a cigarette, as I did, and we blew smoke up towards the sun. Then I heard a strange voice say: "What can Hazel do for you, please?"

I looked over my shoulder. There in the doorway stood a young Malay police officer.

"Just saying hello before I go to see Maureen," I answered.

"Hello." This time it was Hazel, peeping from the side of the doorway. "Please meet my boyfriend, Paul Hassan."

We shook hands. He was a little taller than the usual Malay and good looking with it. I finished my cigarette.

"Are you going to auntie's?" Hazel asked me.

"Yes."

"Maureen will explain when you get there."

"OK," I said, and after shaking hands all round, I waved in a trishaw wallah and went on down to auntie's.

Maureen had seen me from the upstairs window when I was some forty yards from auntie's front step. She must have come down the stairs three at a time.

"Why didn't you tell me you were coming?" she demanded excitedly.

"I didn't know myself until two days ago," I replied. "I came as soon as possible."

"I'll get changed ready for work," she said.

Up to this time, I hadn't given the Piccadilly or her work a single thought. Looking at my watch, I saw it was 7.50 pm. Ten minutes later, I was seated on my usual stool at the bar of the Piccadilly and thirty seconds after that, I was accompanied by a large brandy and Canada Dry.

"You know what that does to me," I said to Maureen, pointing to my glass.

"Yes. But not tonight. It isn't my time. But maybe tomorrow," she said, pushing a glass of water and a little package to the side of the brandy. "Take that later," she ordered.

"OK," I said. "Whatever you say."

She responded with a naughty wink and we smiled at each other.

"That doesn't need any hot water," she explained. "Put it on your

tongue and swallow it with the water. And afterwards, no more brandy
– only beer."

"Yes, ma'am. Thank you, ma'am." It was my turn to give her a
wink.

She smiled and took my hand over the bar. "You're a good friend."

"Thank you for the package."

"You're welcome."

It was about now that I noticed she was dressed in Malay national
costume. Why I hadn't seen it before, I don't know. On asking, she
told me that for some weeks now there had been a new manager and
he wanted national dress for the staff to separate them from the other
"ladies", normally wearing cheongsams.

"A good move," I said, admiring the pattern of brightly coloured
flowers on the two-piece, ankle-length costume.

"You like it?" she asked.

"Beautiful."

She squeezed my hand again. Some beers later when she had to
serve someone else along the bar, I took the opportunity to look at my
watch. It said 10.30. I'd better move fast, I thought. Maureen was now
looking my way. I signalled with my forefinger and she came back to
my end of the bar with another small Tiger.

"Would you like to have a picnic tomorrow?" I asked as she poured.

"Where? When? How?" she said.

"If you can catch a bus to Tanjong Bungah, ask the driver to put
you off at Sandycroft. I'll meet you at the gate. I can hire two bikes
and we can cycle to wherever we want. I can also arrange for a lunch
to be packed ready."

All this seemed to please her. "Do you want another Tiger?" she
asked with a smile.

"No. I'd better be on my way back. I'm not quite sure where I catch
the bus," I lied. "See you tomorrow then?"

She said: "At twelve o'clock. OK?"

"OK." We squeezed each other's hands.

At the door, I looked back and we both held up a hand in farewell.

Next morning, Tug Wilson and I were seated at the breakfast table
in the Leave Centre, reading copies of the *Straits Times*. Bob Raynor
had gone to the office to see if any mail had arrived. We knew that
the Hussars had once again filled the list for the rowing boat so,

breakfast finished, the two of us had a short stroll along the beach. On our return we found Bob sitting on a rock, reading a letter and holding another two beneath it.

"Is that all the mail?" asked Tug.

"Sorry," said Bob. "Just these three." He folded the first letter, put it back in its envelope and opened the next.

We shrugged our shoulders. Sitting on the sand, we watched the wavelets breaking into a soapy froth just short of reaching us. But there wasn't much interest in that, so we looked up at Bob. He was holding something up to his nose, something pale blue.

"What have you got there?" I asked.

"Nothing much really." Sheepishly, he held something which was tied with a pale blue ribbon up to the sun.

"What the hell is that?" I queried.

"It's a present from my pen pal in Australia."

"Give us a shufti!" Tug demanded. Taking the end of the ribbon between thumb and forefinger, he held it a little higher. "It's a short-and-curly!" he exclaimed. "How did you get her to send you one of them?"

"It's in exchange for one of mine," came the reply.

That was Bob Raynor, true as a die. The reader will understand Bob a little better when I explain that I had personally seen in his AB64 Part 1, Bob's "Trade on Enlistment" entered as "Poacher". I believe to this day that he could talk pearls from their oysters.

Leaving Tug and Bob on the beach, I walked through the dining hall. The clock said 11.40. At reception I picked up a hamper. The boy in the stores had already taken two bikes to the gate. I slipped him a twenty-cent note.

"*Terima kasih*," (thank you) he said, touching a finger to his forehead.

After strapping the hamper to the pannier of the larger cycle, I sat on the grass and lit a Rough Rider. It was now 11.55. A bus arrived from Georgetown, stopped a few seconds, then continued on it's way. There on the opposite side of the road stood a vision – white blouse, shorts and sandals. I opened the gate. Smiling, Maureen crossed the road.

"Are we ready?" she asked.

"I couldn't be any readier," I answered, taking hold of my cycle and indicating for her to do the same with the other.

I closed the gate and we were off for our picnic. We cycled for about forty, maybe fifty minutes. To our right we came to a bay which looked very inviting. We walked with our bikes through the shoulder-high shrubbery, coming to an open area free of grass, shrubs and rocks; just dry, silver sand. Couldn't be better!

We leaned our cycles against a shrub at the border. There was a path leading from our sun spot (as it will be called from now on) to the beach and the ocean beyond. Half-way to the water's edge, Maureen let go of my hand and said: "Wait a minute. You go and test the water."

"OK." I had remembered to put on my bathing trunks after my shower that morning. So taking off my shirt, shorts and sandals, into the sea I went, slowing down a little as the waters reached my knees, then waist, then chest. I now turned around. Whatever is she doing? I wondered.

Going back slowly until the water was at waist level, I stopped. There she came out of the shrubs, onto the beach. She had cast off her blouse, shorts and sandals and as she walked towards the water, I could see she was wearing only her "slave chain", which she had previously shown me that night in the Broadway.

The chain was around her waist with the heart-shaped medallion suspended from two small hoops and covering her navel. The medallion was of crimson enamel with fake diamante stones around the outer edge. As I remembered, the reverse side was of silver-plated pewter and engraved in the centre was "Roy's". From a third hoop at the base, an adjustable leather thong passed down between her legs and was fastened to the chain at the small of her back. (The lady who had measured Maureen for her cheongsam at the stall in the Bazaar had since informed me that it was the girls themselves who called these articles "slave chains". She told me it was customary for a girl to buy her own but not so usual for her to have a boy's name engraved on the back. That was very special.)

A nymph, Maureen stood at the water's edge. "You like?" she asked. Too impressed for words, I came further out of the water.

"That's not fair," she said now, pointing at my trunks. Then she put her hands behind her back. I saw the medallion drop a few inches and come to rest on her nest. "Two can play that game," she said simply.

I couldn't argue. So I played the game her way, kicking off my trunks alongside my other things. We made our way back to our sun spot. Maureen searched the hamper and spread out two towels she found there. Also inside the hamper we found two bottles of orangeade, a bowl of cold, boiled rice and another bowl of cooked ham, shrimps and prawns, all of which we knew would make a good *nasi goreng*; a favourite dish. Sitting on the towels, we dipped our fingers in turn and devoured the lot, plus some fruit.

Very satisfied, I lay down to get some sun on my back. Then I felt Maureen's hands brushing the sand off my skin, after which her arm came over my shoulder and I could feel her breasts pressing into me.

"What are you doing?" I asked – as if I didn't know.

"Me? Nothing," she said softly. "But we, in a moment, are going to make love."

I turned over. She lay still and I pretended to brush sand from her body, asking her to turn around.

"Why?" she enquired.

"I want to see how I can get your medallion back to where it was the first time."

She giggled. "OK."

After discovering the other notch on her leather thong, I fastened it to her chain and when she turned over again, the medallion was back covering her navel. Once again I pretended to brush sand from her body.

"You ready now?" She looked deep into my eyes.

"As I ever will be," I said. "Need you ask?"

Some time later, we made a quick dash for the ocean where we sat and washed the sweat off our bodies. Maureen seemed very content.

"You make love good when you have sun on your back," she said now.

"Thank you, ma'am," I said. "I'm not sure if it was the sun or the package you gave me last night."

"What? You didn't take it all last night?"

"No. Only a little on the tip of my tongue. The bigger part I had this morning at breakfast time."

"So it is me who is making you please me, after all?"

"You certainly know what you're doing!"

We both laughed and made our way back to tidy up our sun spot. Then, reluctantly, it was back to Sandycroft, returning the cycles to the stores and the hamper to the kitchen.

We sat waiting at the bus stop; me having a smoke and Maureen another orange drink. She said how much she had enjoyed our picnic. I said that I couldn't have wished for anything better. We could see her bus was coming. Then she did something I had thought impossible for an Eastern lady. She kissed me – there at the bus stop on a main road.

"See you later." She smiled.

"OK." And she was gone.

It was a quiet night at the Piccadilly. We talked a lot as usual. I drank a lot as usual. Then, at about 11 pm, Hazel came in with Paul. The three of them kept talking in Malay. I could feel Paul's and Hazel's eyes on me. At about 11.30, I made my excuses and stood ready to leave. Paul shook my hand and Hazel kissed my cheek. I had already told Maureen that tomorrow I was going rowing with my mate at Sandycroft.

"So, see you tomorrow night, OK?" I reached for her hand and raised it to my lips.

She winked. "Good night," she said. "See you tomorrow."

Bob and I had our turn with the rowing boat, the following day. Unfortunately, we hadn't been told the limit was half an hour and we stayed out on the ocean for a full hour, which didn't go down too well. After that, the leave grew a bit tedious. Cash was getting low. Bob and I visited the Hotel Metropole one night, just to have a free beer with Penang Joe. We had to share the bottle.

On 8 February we returned to Glugor Barracks, and the next day we rejoined A Company who were now at Grik. My memories of Maureen and especially of our beautiful picnic helped to divert my mind from the prospect of jungle-bashing.

41.

Smelly Days

Frank Keenan – Private C Company

Private John Kelly and I were both from Bradford. When 8 Platoon was attached to the Coldstream Guards at Tapah in February 1950, we were Number One and Two on the Bren. We had been on a three-week operation in the Blue Valley of the Cameron Highlands. On getting back to base at Tapah, a weapons inspection was announced before we could have a shower. As our tent had been closed up tight all the time we had been away, you can guess what the heat was like in there – 120 degrees.

After we had stripped off, we just wore our towels round our waists. We hadn't changed our socks all the time we had been on the op. They had dried on us time and again with the water, mud and dirt of the many rivers and streams we had crossed. Our feet were green with the skin dried and wrinkled like prunes, and they stank like ammonia. God, I can smell them now!

When the Second Lieutenant came into the tent to carry out the weapons inspection, he turned red, blue and purple, coughed and spluttered and flew out of the tent, gasping: "What's that ungodly smell?" Then, from a safe distance, he ordered us to report to the Officers' Mess with our weapons after we were showered and all cleaned up.

On another occasion, in August 1950 when the Battalion came into Penang for Rest and Retraining, John Kelly and I were getting showered and changed to go down town. We didn't have any Brylcreem for our hair and nobody would give us any. All we could find was some cooking fat out of a Gurkha ration pack. So we slapped it on and reckoned that we both looked pretty good with hair all slicked down and a big quiff.

Then off we went to Georgetown and had a great time – City Lights, Piccadilly, the New World Bazaar – then back to Minden Barracks and to bed.

Next morning, I awoke to a horrible smell. It was a smell like 100-year-old dead fish in cat's piss! I thought it was coming across from Kelly's bed, so I called him every name I could think of. He screwed up his nose and said it wasn't him – it was me! When some of the other guys woke up, they grabbed us both and threw us in the showers. It turned out that the grease we had put on our hair was fishbone cooking fat that had turned rancid during the night. Well, you can imagine the reaction of the others in the barrack-room!

42.

A Deadly Lesson

Redvers Battersby – Serjeant A Company

Whilst on a two-day patrol in the Baling area early in 1950, I had two officers in my Section who had just joined the Battalion. It was the practice to take new officers out and show them the ropes. I was the Serjeant in charge. They had no power of command and just had to watch. We called them "riders".

Getting on to the end of our first day, I was making for a squatter area I knew in order to bed down for the night. As the scouts broke out of the jungle, they halted the patrol and called for me to come forward. When I did so, I saw that we had emerged into a cleared area which consisted of a valley with a stream at the bottom. On a path on the far side were three men, two of whom were carrying guns. They were about 300 yards away and about the same height as us up the opposite side of the valley.

I deployed the Section in the clearing and told our two Chinese detectives to call to the men to halt or we would fire. This they did, whereupon the three men opposite bolted. I now grabbed the Bren and made the Bren-gunner bend forward to make his back a support for the gun. I then opened fire, using the tracer rounds to get amongst them. I fired off two mags; the Bren-gunner complaining I'd burned his neck with the empties. The three figures dropped in the grass, so I shouted to cease fire and took the Section across the stream and up the other side.

We came across a path and followed it to the place where we'd first seen the three men. There was a lot of blood on the ground and then a trail of it going in the direction that I wanted to go. So off we went. After about 200 yards, we came upon the dead body of a young Malay. I searched him but only found a packet of Rough Riders cigs. I laid him on his face and examined his wounds. He had been hit in the back with a burst from the Bren. We were in a cultivated area, so I got two of the lads to bring a pole. We tied the body to it and set off to find the first hut on our way.

After a while, we reached a hut just before dark. I set up the Bren covering the path, put sentries out and told the other lads to take over the hut and get a meal going, as the occupants had bolted when they'd heard the shooting. Whilst we were having our meal, I told the wireless-man to contact Company HQ. He tried and then said we were in a blind spot but he would try again in the morning. The detectives now said they would try to get back to a nearby village and see if they could contact Baling.

"OK," I said, "but don't come back in the dark, as I've got sentries out with orders to shoot at anything that moves."

Shortly after, when we were settling down for the night, there was a commotion outside. I then found that dogs were trying to eat the body which I'd parked outside as it was beginning to smell. The two new officers were shocked at some of the comments that the lads made. I told them: "Before long, you'll be just as callous as the rest of us!"

Next morning as we were breakfasting, the signaller came over and said to me: "I've got through to HQ and they say we have to stay here till they come with the OCPD (Officer Commanding Police District) from Baling, as all hell's broken loose. It seems that the Malay villagers were saying that the commies had ambushed their headman and head-priest and killed the headman's son. And but for our Chinese detectives stopping them, they were coming to sort the squatter area out!"

"Fair enough," I said, getting the picture. I then told the lads the situation and doubled the sentries.

Anyway, they all came along – Company Commander, OCPD and other bigwigs. I told them what had happened and the outcome was that I had to do an acoustic test. So I went back up the side of the valley with the OCPD to the place where the three men had been when challenged. Our officers crossed to the other side and were nearly at the point where I'd opened fire when I heard the Company Commander say: "We must be near."

So I called: "No, sir. Ten yards to your right."

He looked over, surprised, and said: "Did you hear me?"

When I said I had and so did the OCPD, the test was finished. "I only whispered," the Company Commander said, completely satisfied.

I realised then that my mistake had been telling the Chinese detectives to shout, because with their accent the Malays thought they were commies. Anyway, a month later I was found not guilty by Baling Court and compensation was paid to the headman. But I'm afraid if he had brought his villagers up that path that night, he'd have lost a lot more.

43.

Lost and Found

Gordon Hill – Lance Corporal B Company

In March 1950 our Company base was at Pelam. Early one morning, we set out on a one-day patrol. We proceeded through the tappers' lines and headed towards a small footbridge which crossed a stream at the edge of the jungle.

During the early hours, there had been a monsoon which we found had made the stream into a fast-flowing river. The footbridge was no longer visible, so we made a guess at where it might be. Arthur Bills was the leading scout at this time and I was following. We had guessed correctly. Arthur found the bridge but misjudged the angle of it. As he started to cross, the current was so strong it washed him into the river where we lost sight of him for a short time as he was carried downstream. Luckily, he managed to grab hold of something – a rock or a branch – and held on until a few of us were able to wade in and pull him out. But he had lost his silent Sten gun.

A few days later, we went back to the same spot. The water had now subsided and the Sten gun was recovered. It was in a bit of a state, as you can imagine. Arthur stripped it down to clean it. When he got to the baffles in the silencer, he found it had been slicing bullets in two and only been firing half a bullet at a time; the other halves were still in the silencer!

16. Lance
Corporal Gordon
Hill (left) and
Private Arthur
Bills with his
silent Sten in a
Kedah rubber
estate in 1950.

Arthur had that gun for the rest of his tour out there, but he never liked "the bloody thing" as he called it.

44.

Taiping Hospital

Roy Caldecott – Lance Corporal A Company

Between 1949 and 1951, I was hospitalised six times at the Taiping British Military Hospital, suffering from malaria and dysentery. On 1 March 1950, just three weeks after returning from my leave in Penang, I found myself once again in Taiping BMH with amoebic dysentery.

Six weeks treatment there would be followed by two weeks convalescence in the Cameron Highlands.

In our ward we had three Guards sergeants. One had a dislocated shoulder put back in place. He had received the injury playing rugby. He was a big, red-haired chap, at least six feet, six inches tall and with a chest like a barrel. I thought to myself that I wouldn't have liked to face the chap who had given him the injury!

One morning, the matron was making her daily rounds. "What have you got that tea bucket under your bed for?" she asked one of the sergeants.

"We thought it could do with a good clean," he answered.

"Good for you. It's about time it had a clean."

The bucket in question was filthy. Stain upon stain had built up until there were numerous dark rings around the inside. It was so bad that the sergeants had requested that one of the orderlies bring some emery paper from the hospital maintenance room, along with some old rags and metal polish. For four days they passed the bucket and cleaning materials from one to the other and on the fifth morning, it was back under the bed.

The time came for Matron's daily call and on her orders, out the bucket came. It was like chrome; a real credit to the three sergeants. Matron placed it on the table in the centre of the ward and said: "I have an idea for this."

One hour later, back came the matron escorted by two sisters and an orderly, each of whom was carrying a bunch of flowers. Into the bucket went the brightly coloured blooms; the matron herself making the final arrangement. On her way out, she stopped by the foot of the red-haired sergeant's bed.

"You are the one who woke up the whole hospital when you were admitted, aren't you?" she enquired.

"Yes, Matron. I was having my dislocated shoulder put back in place," he explained, "and I found it very painful."

"Painful? Painful?" said Matron. "What pain do you think your mother went through when she gave birth to you?"

"Point taken," said redhead. "But did she try to have me put back?"

The matron turned and left the ward without further comment.

The following day, 12 March, Lady Mountbatten honoured us with a visit. The flowers in the bucket had been added to and those hanging over the rim were reflected on the bright and shining metal. It made a beautiful show. Lady Mountbatten passed around the ward, having a word here and a word there about our ailments, but not a word from her ladyship about the lovely flower display. We thought that someone would have told her about the work the three sergeants had done.

No, not a word, when just a brief statement of appreciation to the sergeants would have meant so much to all of us. So be it.

Another day, the doctor entered our ward, closely followed by an orderly carrying a kidney-shaped bowl. In the bowl was a sixteen-inch long, chrome tube with a pistol grip and trigger at one end. Stopping at the foot of my bed, the doctor ordered: "Let's have you on your knees on the edge of the bed."

As I obliged, the orderly was covering the tube with vaseline.

"Take a deep breath, please," said the doctor.

Gladly, I thought. My anus was then vaselined and the tube inserted. I learned later that the tube was called a sigmoidoscope and its trigger sent a light into my intestines to see if there was any sign of ulcers. From the patient in the bed opposite – a certain KOYLI corporal called Charlie Chase – came the comment: "You've lost your ring-piece now, Cal!"

I couldn't find an answer. Some minutes later, again from Chase: "Did you like that, Caldy?"

Once more I made no reply but was grateful that the ordeal was over.

Two days later, the same doctor and orderly returned to our ward and the orderly was carrying the bowl as before. Not again! I thought. But instead of coming to me, the orderly pulled the curtain around Charlie Chase's bed. Phew! I then scribbled a note and passed it to the lad to my left and told him to send it round the ward. On the note I had written an instruction of what everyone should do on receiving my signal of one-two-three.

During Charlie's examination, four junior orderlies happened to be walking along the outside verandah.

"Come here, you lot!" called the doctor. "You don't have many opportunities like this, so you might as well learn a little while you have the chance."

In they came and all four of them took it in turn with the pistol grip. I signalled with my fingers: one-two-three. And on three, all nineteen of us joined in loud chorus: "You've lost your ring-piece now, Charlie! Did you like it?"

It was only a matter of days until my six weeks treatment came to an end. I made the short trip to the Cameron Highlands on 1 April, only to find myself in a room with two old friends; one from A Company by the name of "Smiler" Davidson, and the other was the Canadian from C Company, Roy (Nobby) Clarke – both corporals at that time. I was in good company.

45.

Songs

Jock Scurr – Private Signal Platoon

If there was one activity that was even more popular among men of the KOYLI than football, it was drinking. And when they were drinking, they nearly always ended up singing. Well, I was never much good at football and during my early months in Malaya when I was still a non-drinker, I never used to sing either. However, in later times I found that two or three bottles of highly potent Tiger beer could easily induce me to join in with the regular songsters.

One of my pals during the early months was a lad from Batley called Johnny Ainsworth whom I'd known since basic training. Johnny had been a theological student prior to his call-up and planned to become a Church of England clergyman after demob. I've always remembered his favourite joke which went as follows:

A lady teacher was giving a lesson in the classroom when a little girl put her hand up and asked: "Please Miss, do the angels marry in Heaven?"

Whereupon a little boy at the back of the class called out derisively: "Do they fuckin' 'ell!"

To which the teacher responded impatiently: "One question at a time, children, please!"

Anyway, one evening in March 1950, Johnny and myself were seated in the NAAFI in Glugor Barracks, Penang, drinking ice-cold Fanta minerals. At a nearby table, four men, formerly of the Durham Light

Infantry and apparently well oiled on Tiger, suddenly burst forth into a joyous rendering of "The Blaydon Races" and in no time at all, every Geordie in the place enthusiastically joined in. This proved too much for the Yorkshiremen present, all of who, including Johnny, immediately gave voice to "On Ilkley Moor ba't 'at?" The volume of noise was tremendous as each of the two songs alternately rose to ascendency over the general din. As a neutral observer, it seemed to me that the contest was a draw, and both parties eventually appeared to reach the same conclusion and finally gave up amidst considerable laughter and exchanges of good-humoured wisecracks.

Of course, most songs that were sung in NAAFIs, Company canteens and occasionally even in the field were not nearly so respectable. Well, let's face it, most of them were downright filthy! Songs such as "Mary in the garden sifting rice", "Maggie Mae", Reilley's daughter", "That was a cute little rhyme", "Like a good girl should", "All my life I wanted to be a prostitute", "We are the Queen Street girls", "She's a big fat twat", "There was a young lady who walked like a duck" and many more. It was always advisable to be familiar with some of these lyrics in case at some booze-up, a chorus of voices issued you with the ultimatum: "Sing! Sing! Or show your fucking ring!"

Most of the above songs were commonly sung in service camps, bars and sports clubs throughout the English-speaking world, but personally I only ever heard "Mary in the garden sifting rice" whilst in the KOYLI in Malaya where it was very popular in C Company. Because this song may therefore be rare and for personal, nostalgic reasons, I have been sorely tempted to write down here the lyrics of all four verses. But with enormous regret I have reached the conclusion that some of the lines are just too obscene to include in a book like this. Sorry!

There were, however, five "regimental" songs, the words of which I am most anxious to write down. To the best of my knowledge they have never been recorded in print anywhere else and as the surviving members of the Battalion won't be around all that much longer, there is a danger that the words of these songs could be lost forever. The said lyrics are not particularly brilliant but they are nonetheless an important part of Light Infantry history.

When the men of the 2nd Battalion, KOYLI were transported from Deolali in India to Taiping, Malaya, they sailed from Madras. It was in this port that the 1st Battalion, then known as the 51st Regiment of Foot, had landed in 1799 and it was also here that the 2nd Battalion had been raised as the 105th Madras Light Infantry in 1839. The men of the 2nd Battalion duly arrived in Taiping in September 1947 and were impressed by this neat and orderly town with it's cheerful, friendly inhabitants, as well as by the fresh greenery of the surrounding jungle-covered countryside – a stark contrast to the barren plateau of Deolali. From India they brought with them several faithful, long-serving char and dhobi wallahs and also a simple but strangely haunting little ditty which, as far as I ever knew, only had one short verse.

> Oh, Deolali sahib!
> Oh, Deolali sahib!
> Fifteen annas, one rupee;
> Sixteen annas, one buckshee!

I do not know the source of the next song but presume that it may also have originated in a previous era. Like "Deolali sahib", it also appeared to have only one verse, and although it was always sung with rousing enthusiasm, it always seemed to me to be sadly incomplete.

> We are the KOYLI.
> We'll kill the enemy by and by.
> Every man of the regiment
> Is ready to do or die!

Both of these above lyrics had their own original tunes. The next song, however, was sung to the tune of "The Red Flag" which is also the melody of the old American ballad "Maryland, My Maryland". This song hardly reflects the regimental pride of the previous number. It probably originated from some of the men of the 2nd Battalion, Durham LI who were drafted to the 2nd Battalion, KOYLI in 1947. They were certainly the lads who seemed to sing it with most gusto!

> Roll on the day, roll on the hour
> When I will leave this fucking shower.
> Roll on that lovely day when I
> Will leave the KOYLI.
> The Koyli flag is blue, buff, green.
> The biggest bluff you've ever seen.

17.78 Group on 15 December 1949, going home to Blighty. All originated from the 2nd DLI and no doubt would give fervent voice to "Roll on the day, roll on the hour . . ."

> Roll on the day, roll on the hour
> When I will leave this fucking shower!

Then there was a song, the tune of which was very similar to that of the Second World War ditty "Have you heard of a place called Benghazi?" Whoever wrote it appears to have been indulging in some rather wicked wishful thinking regarding his Company Commander!

> I'll sing you a song of Malaya,
> Malaya the land of the sun.
> I'll sing you a song of the jungle
> And the death of a poor mother's son.
> Now a party of Koylis were marching.
> The Bren gun was covering the rear,
> When up spoke the Company Commander
> Who said "It's an ambush, I fear!"
> We took up defensive positions.
> The recce did cover the front,
> And he stood there in the middle

85

> And shouted like a big silly cunt.
> Now he shouted his orders amongst us.
> The bullets did fly round his head.
> He shouted his orders amongst us,
> And soon the poor bastard lay dead.
> We buried him out in the jungle.
> Crossed matchets we placed on his grave,
> And up spoke a certain young Koyli
> And these are the few words he gave.
> "My trade is not parson or preacher.
> These words they do come from my mind,
> That when we do leave this here jungle,
> We'll leave the old bastard behind!"

Finally, there was a much-loved KOYLI nonsense song which was sung with great gusto at every booze-up I ever attended.

> Now they sent us off to Constance to see what we could do.
> Half of us were puddled before six months were through.
> Over the top the Infantry, the Irish Rifles too.
> We all joined in the chorus at the Battle of Waterloo.
> There were RCs, C of Es, Chinese, Japanese,
> Maltese and Standardese and some of the Infantree.
> There were Bombardiers and Brigadiers
> And Mademoiselles from Armetiers,
> Some of the Irish Rifles and the KOYLI!

There were slight variations to the above lyric. The reader may be puzzled by the word "Standardese". I supposed that it was just a nonsense word for a nonsense song. However, George Williams of B Company has drawn my attention to the fact that the line was originally written as "Maltese and Stand-at-ease." I consider that to be far better, but I have written the line down with "Standardese" because that was how I always heard it sung and how I always sang it myself – though only when drunk!

86

46.

Escort to Singapore

Roy Caldecott – Lance Corporal A Company

M y two weeks convalescence in the Cameron Highlands, following
my treatment at Taiping for amoebic dysentery, stretched out to
just over three. Then, on 25 April I was on my way back to Taiping,
via Kamunting, and on the 28th I was back at HQ in Penang. Two
nights later found me on guard duty. Coming off guard at 6.30 am, I
learned I was to accompany our REME Armourer Sergeant – by name
of Everington – on escort to Singapore. We were to exchange ammunition that was outdated and deliver damaged weapons to the Ordnance
Depot for repair. There was to be another chap coming as escort who
would join us at Prai.

We left Penang at 8.15 pm. Our third member was waiting at the
station at Prai where we found that a steel goods wagon had been
allotted for our use – which from now on I will call "our cabin". Having
loaded the arms and ammo into our cabin, our next job was to fill two
five-gallon jerry cans with drinking-water and another with paraffin for
our lamp which Sergeant Everington had kindly brought with him from
his workshop at HQ. Otherwise we would not have had any light.

As our cabin had been standing in a siding in the sun for who knows
how long, the air inside was stifling. There was a sliding door on each
side which we opened about twelve inches. We then hammered wooden
wedges under the ends. The air was better circulated when we were on
the move, but the atmosphere was still sticky. Being part of a goods
train meant that whenever there was a passenger train going north, we
had to pull into a siding to let it pass. These siding pull-ins were the
only times we were able to wash and gain some relief from the
suffocating heat in our cabin. After the driver had topped up the engine
from a water standpipe, we would quickly strip off our shirts, have a
quick douse, rinse our shirts and then climb back into our cabin as the
engine began to lurch forward once more.

On that first night we learned to our extreme discomfort that the gaps left by the wedged-open doors not only circulated the air but also made a freeway for the mosquitoes. A good night's sleep was quite out of the question. When daylight came, we found ourselves stopping at yet another pull-in. While the other two were having their douse, I took a walk in the direction of a nearby kampong, taking my *kukri* with me. Finding a high fern bush, I slashed off three stems of fronds and dragged them back to our cabin.

No time for me to douse before we were on our way. After eyeing the fronds, Sergeant Everington gave me a funny look. "We can't eat them," he said.

"They're not for eating," I answered. "I thought we could take turns tonight punkahing."

"Punkahing?" He frowned.

"Yes," I insisted. "We can change over every two hours. While two sleep, the third can keep off the mossies by fanning with the fronds. At least we could give it a try."

"So be it," said the Sergeant with a shrug.

We arrived at Kuala Lumpur at noon and learned it would be nine hours before our train would depart. So we closed the doors to our cabin, secured them with padlocks and made our way into town. We found the Galloway Club, introduced ourselves and headed straight for the showers. Joy at last! We asked one of the Indian attendants to buy three cheap shirts for us, but in the meantime, dressed in towels, we enjoyed a Tiger at one end of a secluded bar while we had our clothes laundered but not starched.

At 10.30 pm (one and a half-hours late) we were once again heading for Singapore. The fern fronds turned out to be useful as I had envisaged. Not much fun for the one who was punkahing but the others did get some sleep. The swarms of mosquitoes were held at bay.

After several pull-ins to sidings, we arrived at Singapore at 11.30 am on 3 May and were unloaded at the Ordnance Depot by 3 pm. Sergeant Everington had a load of paperwork to do, so he let me and the other lad loose on the town. We soon found the Union Jack Club and once again we headed straight for the showers. We booked beds for the night and I had a short haircut. After a good dinner and a short walk around town, we bedded down at about 10 pm for a much-needed good night's kip.

The following morning saw us back at the Ordnance Depot. There was more paperwork for Sergeant Everington which he finished by 11.30 am. We then started to check our goods for return. Everything was OK, so off we went back to our cabin. To our annoyance, we found that someone had taken our lamp. It definitely wasn't one of us, so back to Ordnance went our Sergeant. It took him four hours to explain to the QMS what one of his guys must have done and to eventually retrieve the lamp.

We left Singapore at 6 pm as scheduled. After the usual pull-ins, we had our douses. Otherwise the trip back was uneventful. We arrived back at Glugor Barracks, Penang at 11.30 pm the following night and I was glad to get my back on a mattress – even if it was lousy. After that extremely uncomfortable trip, I felt like I needed another three weeks' convalescence.

47.

A Fortuitous Ache

John Kitchen – Private KOYLI Draft

In April 1950 I had almost completed my jungle training and with the rest of my Draft had just finished a patrol from Kroh to Klian Intan, when I began to experience quite bad toothache. We stayed in Klian Intan overnight and returned to Kroh by gharry the following day where I promptly reported sick. The A Company medic gave me a tincture to ease the pain but it had little effect. When CSM Taylor, who was in charge of jungle training, saw my swollen gums, he agreed that I should return to Glugor Barracks in Penang for an examination by the RADC dentist (a captain whose name I forget) in the garrison hospital.

As luck would have it, the next day was Friday and CSM Taylor and Serjeant Broadbent were returning to Penang in the armoured 15-cwt truck for a weekend with their wives. The road from Kroh as far as Baling was designated "red", hence the armoured truck. We were without any escort and stopped only once to relieve ourselves, but the trip continued without incident. We arrived at Glugor Barracks quite late in the day and I was told to report to the hospital MI Room on the following morning, which was Saturday. This I did; only to learn that the dentist had gone for the weekend.

The pain in my tooth receded substantially on that Saturday night and I was able to eat on Sunday. I appeared at the dental office first thing Monday morning and saw the dentist at last. He said I had suffered from a large abscess which had burst on the Saturday, and he had to remove the offending large molar. He checked out my other teeth and said they were in reasonable condition but as he was not very busy, he suggested that over the next few days he should do several fillings. Consequently, he squared the position with CSM Taylor who was returning to Kroh that afternoon to conduct the final week of my Draft's training.

So I spent most of that week in the dentist's chair. On the last day of my repair schedule, he said he would like me to be in his chair at 11 am on the following Monday for a final clean and polish. When that day came, I learned that he was being inspected by the RADC Colonel from NMSD in Taiping and that all the dental Captain's benevolence in caring for my teeth revolved around the fact that he wanted to show what a good job he was doing for the teeth of 1st KOYLI!

We both won out, in that he was given a very good report and I missed the last week of my jungle training.

48.

Boozer's Progress

Jock Scurr – Private Signal Platoon

Like quite a few young lads of my generation, I had only rarely tasted alcohol prior to my call-up into the Army. I remember how perplexed I was at Christmas 1949 in the Light Infantry Brigade Training Centre in Bordon, Hampshire, as I watched drunken young soldiers reeling around the place, speaking incoherently and spewing up the contents of their insides, and the following morning holding their heads and their stomachs and moaning and groaning. What a lot of silly asses! I thought to myself. Why on earth do they do it?

Consequently, when I first arrived in Malaya, it never occurred to me that I would become a silly ass too. Travelling up on the night train from Singapore to Kuala Lumpur, I was so hot and weary that when a mate handed me a half-full bottle of Tiger beer, I drank it down and later noted in my journal that it was "really lovely". Even so, I had no thought of drinking the stuff on a regular basis.

My next encounter with alcohol occurred after I had completed my jungle training and been posted to the Signal Platoon. On Friday night, 31 March 1950, I took a bus into Georgetown with two friends who had both transferred from the King's Royal Rifle Corps to the KOYLI and had done their jungle training with my Draft; namely, Ron Stringer (Signals) and Lance Corporal Berry (MT). We decided to go to see John Wayne's latest epic, *She Wore a Yellow Ribbon*, which was being shown at the Odeon in Penang Road. As we entered the cinema, there was a small, semicircular bar at the left of the foyer.

"Let's have a drink," Ron suggested. "What are you having, Jock?"

I hesitated, not having the slightest notion of what should be drunk at such a time. In desperation I replied: "Well, what are you going to have?"

"I think I'll have a gin," Ron stated.

"Right," I said. "I'll have that as well."

Ron ordered and the very attractive Chinese barmaid served up three glasses of gin. My next problem was figuring out exactly how I should drink it. So I watched Ron as he raised his glass to his lips and knocked the contents back with a quick flick of the wrist. So that's how it's done, I thought. I then put the glass to my lips and tossed the gin back into my mouth. The immediate result was that my throat burned, my eyes watered and I coughed and spluttered uncontrollably! My two companions were highly amused and the young Chinese barmaid nearly had hysterics. Very red faced, I was glad to proceed into the darkness of the picture hall.

After the show, we went over the road to the Broadway Cafe where we had a very nice meal of ham, eggs, chips and coffee. While eating, we all agreed that although the film had been quite spectacular, we were disappointed that it hadn't contained a decent battle scene. Berry then returned to one of his favourite themes – trying to persuade me that I should sign on as a Regular. When we'd finished our coffee, Berry and Ron decided they'd each have a brandy. Following my earlier embarrassing experience with gin, I was very reluctant, so Berry suggested that I try a particular port that he could guarantee I would enjoy. I assented to this and after Berry had had an argument with the Chinese waiter to the effect that the port in the bottle he brought was the wrong colour for the brand shown on the label, I eventually drank a glassful and whether it was the right brand or not, I found it quite pleasant.

Then came Sunday 30 April. My cousin John Kitchen, from Wallsend-on-Tyne, had been undergoing his jungle training at Kroh but had returned to HQ for dental treatment. That Sunday afternoon, John and I went into Georgetown for a stroll around and ended up at the Chinese Town Hall NAAFI to have refreshments. As we entered the place, I glanced to my right and noticed three Regular soldiers who had been with me in Holding Company in Bordon and had subsequently sailed to Malaya with my Draft on the *Devonshire*. "Jungle Jim" (a teller of tall stories) his mate Bert Marsh and old Jim Walters were seated over by the wall at a table that was littered with dead Tiger bottles.

The very drunk Jungle Jim spotted us and loudly bellowed: "Outside, lemonade wallahs!"

It seemed to me that every soldier in the place looked up from his glass of beer and stared at us. We nevertheless continued to the counter and ordered up two glasses of orange crush! This happening really brought home to me the salient factors of barrack-room culture. If you didn't smoke, swear or fornicate, you were decidedly odd; but if you didn't drink, you were like something from outer space!

Anyway, on our return to Glugor Barracks, we adjourned to the NAAFI there and John had another orange drink and I had a cream soda. To our surprise, we met two chaps from Wallsend who joined us at our table and insisted on buying us each a Tiger. By the time I had drunk two-thirds of the large bottle, I felt a trifle giddy but I was also aware that I felt very happy. And it wasn't just the alcohol-inspired feeling of well-being that pleased me. That brown bottle with the famous "tiger and palm tree" motif on the label, standing on the table before me, seemed to me to be a status symbol that proclaimed to all the other soldiers that I belonged – I was one of the lads.

And that is how I started out on the road to becoming a boozer. During the remainder of 1950, I progressed from the occasional Tiger to the not so occasional couple of Tigers and then to the intermittent two or three Tigers. By the early months of 1951, I had become an almost nightly drinker and often behaved like the silly ass that I'd always sworn I'd never be. I now and again drank Tuborg, Anchor or Carlsberg but I liked Tiger best. I remember CSM Potts once said that a couple of bottles of that potent brew made you feel that heaven was yours and that three or four bottles made you believe you owned all of hell as well! I think that just about sums it up.

When in May 1951 an NCO of the Signal Platoon made it plain that he considered me to be a bloody nuisance because I came back from the NAAFI pissed almost every night, I knew then that I had finally made it and was truly fulfilling my role as a Private soldier! Although today my stomach will no longer tolerate large amounts of booze, I am nonetheless eternally grateful to barrack-room culture and Tiger beer for having converted me into a silly ass when I was young. Otherwise, look at all the fun I would have missed!

49.

Ambushers Routed

Charlie McAllister – Lance Corporal C Company

Soon after my return to Malaya for a second tour early in 1950, I was the NCO in charge of a road escort for the Platoon Commander who was returning in his car to 8 Platoon's base at Grik. We had a Ferret scout car and a 3-tonner truck. I was in the cab of the truck with the driver while the others were in the back, armed with a Bren, Stens and rifles.

As we were about to set off, the scout car was found to have broken down, so the Lieutenant decided we should leave without it. When we were about half-way to Grik, it started raining very heavily. The truck had no covering on the back, so the men were having a hard time trying to keep dry and keep a lookout at the same time.

Just as we were passing through a small cutting, we were fired on from the right bank. The men in the back of the truck replied with very rapid and heavy firing. We speeded up out of the ambush; then stopped and dismounted. I moved the men into the trees until we were at the terrorists' rear. We then advanced in extended line, firing as we moved.

When we reached the road, the terrorists had gone, leaving plenty of empty cartridge cases at their ambush position. So we went back to the truck and found a lot of bullet-holes on the side and front of it, and the radiator had also been hit and was useless.

We had to wait for a long time before a search party found us. Fortunately, none of us had been hit in the exchange of fire, but I don't know about the bandits.

50.

On the Road to Grik

Frank Keenan – Private C Company

One day in May 1950 we were escorting Captain Haddon and his batman who were travelling in the Captain's green Vauxhall car, carrying the payroll for 8 Platoon detachment at Grik. The escort truck met them at the Kuala Kangsar – Bahru crossroads. We stopped in Lenggong for a rest and then set off for Grik. In the cab of the truck were the driver, Private Harrison, and Lance Corporal McAllister, i/c escort; and Privates Lloyd, Eathorne, Carter, Swalwell and myself were in the back. It started to rain, so we all huddled up against the cab for shelter.

Half-way between Lenggong and Grik, the bandits opened fire on us from the bank, hitting the front of the truck. Some of the bullets just missed Harrison and McAllister. Of course, the bandits couldn't see the rest of us huddled behind the cab. I managed to grab the Bren gun and fired back almost immediately which took them completely by surprise. Then everybody else opened fire.

The truck came to a halt and we all dismounted and tried to do a flanking attack round the back of them. However, we should have left someone with the truck watching the road. While we were flanking, the bandits crossed the road and escaped. We were pretty shook up and fired into any suspicious-looking bush, but we soon realised they had given us the slip. We found the Vauxhall car round a bend in the road abandoned, with no sign of Captain Haddon or his batman anywhere.

We got back in the truck and Private Harrison drove off, but a few miles up the road the engine burst into flames. So we left the truck and commandeered a Chinese guy's car in which we returned to Grik and reported what had happened.

Captain Haddon and his batman showed up next morning with a large police escort. Their story was that they heard the firing, thought we were dead and took off to get help!

51.

Ampang, 10 June 1950

James Harper – Private D Company

On that fateful day, I was no longer with 10 Platoon and was in fact at the Company base back in Ipoh. But here is an account of the ambush as it was told to me.

The Platoon was then about eighteen to twenty strong and had two serjeants – Serjeant Phil Hogan and newly promoted Serjeant Benny Cookson. In the vicinity of Ampang, they were scouting at the head of D Company when they came to a fork in the track. So Serjeant Hogan decided to split the Platoon into two sections. He would take one section and Serjeant Cookson the other.

Serjeant Hogan's Section set off down one fork of the track and walked right into the ambush. The waiting bandits were hidden in scrub and grass both on high ground and at ground level. I am not certain as to who was leading scout at that time but I rather think it was Private Charlie Harrison, a lad I had trained as a scout before I left the Platoon. I am sure someone said that Harrison and Gough were shot at point-blank range. Anyway, it was all over in a minute or so with both of them, as well as Jones, Boden, Hall and Hudson, all killed. The four others were all wounded. Lance Corporal Vernon (Bomber) Brown later recounted that as he lay on the ground, he saw a bandit jump down from a position on the high bank and walk towards him. Despite his wounds, he had the presence of mind to keep one hand on his rifle and as the bandit came close, Vernon reared up and shot him dead.

Although badly wounded, Serjeant Hogan staggered back to the rest of the Company. The other section of 10 Platoon, under Serjeant

18. The men of D Company bury their six dead at Batu Gajah cemetery on 11 June 1950, after the ambush at Ampang the previous day.

Cookson, apparently were in a position to see Hogan's patrol but were unable to render any immediate assistance. They had to retrace their steps back to the fork in the track and then on to the scene of the ambush. Two others still alive, although wounded, were Privates Storey and Daniels. Storey had his kneecap blown off and Daniels later had to have his right hand and wrist amputated.

It is strange how, a day or so later, poor Vernon Brown was able to describe the incident quite clearly. But as the reaction set in, he just could not close his eyes and sleep without having nightmares about it. Sadly, he died one week later.

52.

Ampang

I am grateful to Fred Sparkes, former Corporal of B Company, for sending me this poem. Originating from the latter half of 1950, it is almost certainly the work of D Company's regular poet and indomitable

soldier, Corporal "Pecker" Green. It is a poem written from the heart
that expresses so clearly our feelings at that time. – J Scurr

'Twas that day in June remember
When those ten men met their grief.
'Twas those days you will remember
When life was very brief.

Into Dead Man's Walk they went
No bandits did they hear.
'Twas then that they did meet them
When the Bren guns opened fire.

Six men were killed and four had wounds
Then the bandits turned and fled.
They did not go unscathed though
For Bomber shot one dead.

Bomber went off to dock then
The doctors did their best.
But Bomber was thinking of Heaven
So we laid him there to rest.

Take heed of this rhyme my brothers
Be careful where you tread.
Just think of the other seven
Before taking that step ahead.

The day will come for vengeance
The Yorkshires will be there.
Those bandits will find us a menace
And we'll drive them from their lair.

Now this is the end of my story
Those lads had bags of pluck.
They fought for Britain's glory
And I wish them all good luck.

53.

Ambush at Ampang

Sid Grant – Lance Corporal Signal Platoon

During my tour of over three years with the KOYLI in Malaya, I spent a lot of my time as a signaller and most of that with D Company, hearing and seeing quite a few things which made you realise that the war in Malaya was not a game. One of the worst things in my experience was the ambush at Ampang, near Ipoh, on 10 June 1950.

I remember on that day we had moved out as a Company to patrol a tin mine area which was called Dead Man's Gully. We went so far by transport and then continued on foot along a track where we halted and set up a Company HQ. From there the patrols went out to search the area, leaving the Company Commander and a few of us in base.

During the time that the patrols were out, we collected a few locals whom we held as suspects for questioning. Not long after, we heard a considerable amount of small arms firing for a short time and then everything went quiet.

The first thing we knew about what had happened was when one of the lads who was a scout for the other patrol came back to us. He was raving about lads being killed and wounded after being caught in the ambush, but did not seem to know any figures. The lad was so bitter we had to calm him down, as he started to threaten the suspects we had collected with his Sten gun, pointing it at them and calling them all the bastards under the sun. He eventually calmed down and went back to the scene of the ambush with the Company Commander and part of HQ.

I had to try to make contact with rear HQ on my wireless. The problem was that they were not due to open up on Battalion net at that time. The only thing I could do was open up and net into another station and hope that they would get our Battalion to open up, which is what happened. The Hussars not only passed the message on but they also turned up at the scene in some scout cars. I was soon able to pass the

19. Private W J Boden of 10 Platoon, D Company stands behind Sid Grant's "68" set during an operation near Ipoh in May 1950, just a couple of weeks before his death in the Ampang ambush.

information back to rear HQ that we had six lads killed and four wounded.

We returned to Ipoh where we were staying with the Gurkha Rifles in their camp. All the lads in the Company were upset over the whole thing. We could not undo what had been done, but I know some promises were made that day.

On the day of the funeral, the CSM of D Company told me I could not attend as someone had to maintain wireless communication. But he asked me if, in between transmissions, I would take some cigarettes and a few other items to the three lads in the hospital. I knew that Lance Corporal Vernon Brown was badly wounded and it made me think that it was not many months before that Vernon and myself had been on RSM Tanner's NCO's Cadre. We both got our first stripe on the same day.

On going into hospital to see the lads, Vernon Brown and Storey were in a bad way and not wanting to talk or wanting anything, which was understandable after what they had gone through. The thing that brought tears to my eyes was to see Private Daniels propped up in bed with a writing-pad, trying to write a letter with his left hand after losing his right in the ambush.

That's the sort of guts that beat the Communists in the end, and I was one of the many who were proud to serve with such men and to be a part of the KOYLI.

54.

Luck, Tragedy and Harmony

Peter Peace – Private D Company

To this day I think how lucky I was regarding the ambush at Ampang in June 1950. When I joined D Company after my jungle training, I was given the Bren gun for 10 Platoon. This I carried through the jungle for some considerable time and, of course, it was three times the weight of a rifle. In the end, the only way I could get the Bren passed on to someone else was to become batman to Lieutenant Green.

At the time of the ambush, Mr Green and myself were down near Singapore. He was on a course with pack-mules to assess the possibility of their use in the jungle. On our return to our quarters at Ipoh, we were told how 10 Platoon had been ambushed. But for that trip south, both of us would, of course, have been on that patrol. The lad who had taken over my Bren gun was Private Daniels whose right arm was so badly shot, it had to be amputated.

However, I was on another patrol, a month later, when Second Lieutenant Pyemont was shot and killed by our own sentry. I can remember the single shot ringing out in the dark and the rest of us being on stand-by for the next hour. The thing I remember most about the shooting is that the sentry, a lad from Newcastle or Sunderland, didn't seem a bit upset by it all. I think it would have affected me.

Although hard at the time and dangerous, they were happy days. We were all young lads together, all living in a foreign land far from home, but I cannot recall many of us falling out. Perhaps the world would be a better place these days if people could live together in harmony as we all did in the KOYLI in Malaya.

55.

Into the Inferno

Ron Stringer – Private Signal Platoon

A bout two weeks after the Ampang ambush in June 1950, a report was received of a bandit group camped in the area south of Dead Man's Gully. It was arranged that the other three rifle companies would be used as stops, taking up ambush positions around the location, and following an air strike on the predicted bandit position, D Company would make a sweep through the area and hopefully get revenge for our recently fallen comrades. I had been allocated to D Company as a

20. D Company HQ personnel in the Lenggong jungle in July 1950. The variety of regimental origins in the Battalion is very evident here. (Left to right) ex-Ox and Bucks LI, ex-DLI, ex-KSLI, Ron Stringer ex-KRRC, ex-DCLI and KOYLI.

signaller only a week before. There was considerable anger among the lads and a determination to get their own back on the bandits.

On the day of the operation we took up position, about forty strong, at the edge of the jungle. Brigands and Tempests bombed and strafed the area before us. Then, in we went. It was terrifying! The jungle was on fire all around us. We struggled through the rocket-blasted trees and foliage as the flames continued to encircle us. We saw no bandits and were, in fact, lucky to escape with our lives.

When we emerged from that inferno, miraculously without any casualties, our relief was only matched by our disappointment that we'd made no contact with the enemy.

56.

Jungle Quest

Jock Scurr – Private Signal Platoon

We fill up our glasses with cold Tiger beer
And think of the lads who are no longer here.
A safe journey home is what every man craves,
But bugles have blown over young soldiers' graves.

Such sombre thoughts never linger for long.
Soon they're dispelled by a joke and a song.
Then it's early to bed, to rest while we may,
For we're off on a duffy the following day.

When we enter the jungle, we soon start to climb
Through bamboo and attap and rattan and slime.
We sweat and we curse 'neath the weight of our packs,
While the Dyak up front follows two-day-old tracks.

Breathless we stumble on up to the crest
Of each hill we climb, but there's no time for rest.
Our officer whispers that bandits are near,
But our own gasping lungs are all that we hear.

Exhausted and thirsty we constantly squeeze

21. Struggling uphill through dense jungle, bearing a full pack, was an arduous, sweat-soaked, totally exhausting ordeal.

> Beneath hanging creepers and branches of trees,
> Bruised by tree-trunks and saplings and plants
> And bleeding from leeches and thorns and red ants.
>
> We now start to wonder if our weary plight
> Will leave us in any condition to fight.
> Then just as we're all about ready to drop,
> We're suddenly given the signal to stop.
>
> The scouts give the sign that a camp's up ahead.
> Just minutes from now a mate might lie dead.
> The prospect of losing a comrade is grim,
> But no man admits it could also be him.
>
> Our officer leads an immediate attack.
> We level our weapons and creep up the track.
> But the bashas are empty, the bandits have flown.
> Vain moments of hope are all we have known.
>
> A short halt for tiffen, then on with the chase.
> But rain swamps the tracks, so we stop to make base.

103

We build three-man bivvies and cook all-in stew
And drenched by the rain we enjoy a hot brew.

Though plagued by mosquitoes and cramped, cold and wet,
We lie in our bivvies and hope to sleep yet.
And finally when into slumber we sag,
We're rudely awakened to go out on stag.

Facing the track in the dark jungle night,
The sentry is sitting alone with his fright.
Shrill wailing and roaring and screeching he hears,
And the moving black shadows all add to his fears.

Patrols on the second day search for fresh tracks,
Thankfully minus the loads on our backs.
But the jungle hills still leave us battered and worn,
With uniforms sweat-soaked and mud-stained and torn.

When the final day dawns, we pack and depart.
It's a long trek back home and we're tired from the start.
For three days we've searched the dank jungle in vain.
Our murderous foes have escaped us again.

We fill up our glasses with cold Tiger beer
And think of the lads who are no longer here.
A good sleep tonight and two days of rest,
Then we're back to the bush to continue the quest.

57.

Abandoned in Haste

Gordon Hill – Lance Corporal B Company

After our tour at Pelam, the Company moved to Batu Gajah before going on the fourteen-day Lenggong duffy in which the full Battalion took part in July 1950. Each company had it's own area to patrol. After a few days, B Company had an air drop of rations and we built a base camp to patrol from.

One day, a small patrol of about six or eight of us, with Serjeant Lynn in charge, pushed on through the jungle and came across a disused rubber plantation. We then followed a stream which led us to a Communist camp that would have accommodated about 100 personnel. They must have had word of us coming as they had left in a hurry, leaving food cooking and coffee boiling on the fires. It was a well organised camp with washing facilities and clothes-lines.

A few days later, after our second air drop, we found a small camp close by which had housed about four Communists. We thought they might have been runaways from the main camp. It may have been the noise of the planes making the air drop that warned them to move on.

After Lenggong, we went into Penang for Battalion bullshit during the Rest and Retraining period.

58.

The Last Columns

Jock Scurr – Private Signal Platoon

Towards noon on Thursday 20 July 1950, I was marching with C Company across an extensive grassed hillside, somewhere to the east of the River Perak. We had just left the jungle and entered this stretch of open hill country. Consequently, I had a rare opportunity of being able to view the whole Company on the march, instead of only the man before me as was customary on jungle operations.

Immediately in front of me was Arthur Greenacre, loaded up like a mule with a satchel and rolled poncho cape roped on top of his weighty "68" set. A little ahead of Arthur, I could see the "Mad Major" Murray striding determinedly, despite his hangover. Ahead of Company HQ, 8 Platoon stretched in a long line of jungle-green figures, plodding diagonally across the hillside. I could easily spot Frank Keenan with his heavy Bren gun slung in front of him and the ammunition pouches on his hips bulging with full magazines. Further ahead, I could distinguish the large and bulky frame of the former "tramp", Joe Costello, and I could pick out Mac McAllister by the way he wore his jungle hat with the brim pulled down all around his head. At the head of the column, behind the two scouts, strode the sturdy figure of the new Second Lieutenant Crisp, fresh from Sandhurst. Glancing behind me, I had a quick view of tall Second Lieutenant Wride and the men of 9 Platoon following in file behind Company HQ.

As we continued up the gradual slope, I was very weary, parched with thirst and finding the searing heat of the overhead sun extremely disagreeable. Yet I became strangely uplifted by a sudden vision of being a part of history – not just the history that we were currently making at that time of the Malayan Emergency. It was more a realisation that I was a living component of one of the thousands of marching columns of British Infantry who, in tunics of red, khaki and green, had during three centuries tramped under a hot sun over inhospitable terrain in British-administered lands throughout Asia and Africa.

Well, the Second World War had rung the death knell of the British Empire and, for better or for worse, a very different world was emerging. I was only grateful that I had been born just in time to be a part of those marching columns before they were no more.

59.

My Lucky Escapes

George Hodgson – Private D Company

At the end of July 1950 when the Battalion had withdrawn into Penang for two months, I was out one night with my comrades at the City Lights dance hall and very much enjoyed our outing.

As we were leaving to go back to camp, the monsoon rain was very heavy. We were all the worse for drink and could hardly see where we were going in the rainstorm. When we started to run to catch a taxi, I slipped and fell over into a monsoon drain which was overflowing with the torrents of rain. The rushing flow of water was so deep it came up to my neck and for an awful moment I thought I was going to drown.

Luckily, I somehow managed to grab the bank of the drain and was able to lift myself out with the help of my mates, who were as drunk as I was. Then, we all struggled into a taxi; all of us dripping wet, especially me. I just kept thinking that I'd had a narrow escape from death.

I had another close shave eight months later, in March 1951. The Company was stationed at Kroh and 10 Platoon had just returned from a jungle patrol. After our rifles were inspected by our officer, we were dismissed to our tents. While we were resting on our beds, one of my comrades was cleaning his rifle and suddenly it went off. A bullet shot through my mate's soap-box and just missed my leg.

These were two of my unforgettable experiences while serving in the Far East with the KOYLI.

60.

Laughter All Round

Gordon Hill – Lance Corporal B Company

During Battalion Rest and Retraining in Penang in August 1950, one of the privates from 4 Platoon went down town and unknowingly wandered into a brothel where he was picked up by the Military Police. They sent him back to camp with orders to report to an NCO.

When he came to me, I questioned him – in my capacity as Lance Corporal – about what he had done. He said he had only been having a drink of orange in what he thought was a bar, but there were a lot of girls smiling at him. (He was a bit dim!) Then, he said, the MPs came in and grabbed him. When I then asked him if that was all he had to report to an NCO, he answered yes, so I told him that as he had reported to me, he could go back into town.

He duly had to appear on Company Commander's Orders but when told the story, the Major just laughed and let him off with a caution.

Four months later, when we were stationed at Kroh, we were visited by a Roman Catholic priest who had come to give a service for the Catholics in the Company. So Major Sutcliffe took it upon himself to round up all the Catholics he could find. While searching through the camp, he spotted Private Roberts coming out of the cookhouse in performance of his day's duty as Dining Room Orderly.

"Roberts!" Major Sutcliffe called. "Are you an RC?"

"No, sir," Roberts replied. "I'm a DRO!"

61.

A Lady at Last

Roy Caldecott – Lance Corporal A Company

It may have been August 1950 in Minden Barracks, Penang. One night coming out of the shower, I passed three of our lads going in. After drying myself and sitting on my bed wrapped in my towel – which was the norm – I was cracking open a clean shirt. (This last phrase may have to be explained to any reader unfamiliar with the stiff-as-a-board starching of the flying dhobi!) The three lads re-emerged and one of them said to one of the other two: "Tell him what you have just told us." This lad then sat on the opposite bed.

"Well?" I said, a little offhandedly.

"I went with a lady last night," he responded.

"You did what?"

"I didn't want to be left out, so I went with a young lady."

"I hope you went to the clinic after?" I asked him.

"Oh yes," was his reply.

"Then what's your problem?"

"Doesn't it make your knees sore!"

He lifted his towel above his knees and I could see that the skin had been chafed off.

"How the hell did you get like that?" I demanded.

"It was the coconut matting."

My gob was smacked. "You mean the matting on the floor?"

"That's right."

My next question had to be asked. "Was there no bed in the room?"

"Oh yes," he replied. "But it looked so neat and tidy and I didn't want to upset it. After all, she did have to sleep there."

He took the biscuit! "You don't have long to go now, do you?" I asked.

"Five days," he replied.

"You've gone all this time without weakening and now, within days of sailing home, you have finally visited a lady." I paused. "And did you like it?"

"Oh yes," he said very earnestly.

I was now standing, having put on my shirt and slacks, readying myself to call on my Maureen at the Piccadilly. The lad stood up facing me. I took him by the shoulders.

"I want you to promise me one thing," I said. "When you get home and you're dressed in your uniform, I want you to look in the mirror, gaze upon the medal ribbon on your breast and say to yourself, 'I earned that. Cal said so'."

And I meant it. I knew we all deserved our ribbons, especially the conscripts. They hadn't asked to be soldiers but they'd done all the things we Regulars had, and done them well too.

Can we all say that we earned our ribbons? Of course we can! We earned them and we deserved them. God bless us all!

62.

Looking Back With a Smile

Peter Peace – Private D Company

Lieutenant Green was a lovely man but not really cut out for the jungle. He was so well known for falling over that if we were, say, crossing a log over a stream, the people in front would walk backwards to see him fall in. As his batman, I always carried a long, thin stick to push the mud out of his rifle barrel. On one patrol in the Ipoh area early in 1950, we made camp on a small hill. In the morning after breakfast, we were all packing up to continue our patrol. Suddenly, Lieutenant Green slipped as only he could do and slid from top to bottom down the hill on his mapcase, causing great amusement to all of the Platoon. But I must say, it was an honour to have been his batman.

My next story happened during Battalion Retraining in Penang in August 1950. One chap in our barrack-room would always go to bed about 9 pm. So one night we decided to play a prank on him. We all started doing our normal early morning routine, sweeping the floor, making our beds, walking into the washroom with towels round our necks, etc. We then woke him up and told him he had slept in. The scenario was so convincing he had a wash and shave before the penny dropped.

Throughout my time in Malaya, my best pal was Stan Smith who was from Oxford like myself. After Battalion Retraining, Major Harding asked me to take over the running of our Company Officers' Mess. Most nights during the period that followed, Stan would bring me a couple of warm Tiger beers and I would give him cold ones from the fridge in the Mess. This went on for some time until one night, I think at a place called Kulim early in 1951, Stan met up with another pal from Oxford. One Tiger led to another and another and at the end of the night, Stan crawled back to his tent up the monsoon ditch, only to find next morning that he was covered from head to toe in green slime!

63.

Bullets and Hornets

Gordon Hill – Lance Corporal B Company

After leaving Penang in September 1950, 4 Platoon, B Company was sent to Klian Intan to guard the tin mine. Once a week on a rota basis, an NCO and two men were invited to the mine for drinks and a game of snooker.

The night I went, the mine was attacked and there was some gunfire. Thankfully, the rest of the Platoon were on the scene within minutes. Among them was the best Bren-gunner in the Battalion – we thought so, anyway – Charlie Kay, who appeared very smartly dressed.

"Tha looks smart, Charlie," I said to him.

"I ought to. I've been in your kit-box!" was his reply.

No one was injured and the only damage was a few bullet-holes in one of the buildings. I think it was a quick hit and off, as they did not like facing the KOYLI. We then returned to camp where I retrieved my kit from Charlie Kay.

A few nights later, we laid an ambush on the Klian Intan to Kroh road. We were out all night and returned next morning without incident.

22. Lance Corporal Gordon Hill of 4 Platoon, B Company at Klian Intan in October 1950. Private Johnson in window.

All of us were laid out on our beds, trying to snatch a brief rest, when Major Doyle, the Company Commander, arrived. He quickly had us all outside and gave us a lecture, telling us he was going to turn night into day as we would be on duty for twenty-four hours. (This turned out to be Private Derrick Snell's favourite story, even to this day.)

So the next morning, after receiving information that the Communists were still in the area, we were issued with three days' rations, two bandoliers of ammunition per man and the NCOs with hand-grenades, and we set off on patrol. As scouts, Arthur Bills and I took the lead. We walked out of the camp and down a track into a small section of jungle where we had to cut our way through. On reaching the far side of this patch of jungle bordering the rubber, we noticed a large hornets' nest hanging from a branch. We warned everybody of this, and all avoided the nest except one idiot at the back of the patrol who decided to chop it down.

Swarms of angry, buzzing hornets immediately attacked. A lot of the lads were stung; some of them so badly that they passed out and had to be carried back, needing medical attention. The Platoon Officer and Serjeant sought refuge by wading out into a small lake. Arthur Bills and I ran up the adjacent hill into the rubber where I slipped and lost a grenade off my belt. But in the confusion, I didn't notice this loss until I got back to camp and was supposed to hand the grenade in. I was now told that I had two choices – go back and look for it or be put on a charge. Arthur and I then went back to the rubber and luckily found the grenade straight away.

After our six weeks at Klian Intan, we went on to Kroh, changing over with 5 Platoon. During our short stay at Kroh, there were not many incidents. We spent Christmas there and did a few patrols between Kroh and Klian Intan.

One day, Gordon Hill, MT scout car driver, asked me, Gordon Hill (Are you confused? The Army certainly was!) to go with him as escort for an ambulance going down to Baling. On the way, the ambulance was fired on. I opened up with the twin Bren guns mounted on top of the scout car, aiming into the bank where I thought the firing was coming from. But I had forgotten to close the hatch and some of the hot, spent casings went down between Gordon Hill's back and the back of his seat. I have never seen a scout car travel so fast!

I had known Gordon previous to going into the Army and we remained good friends until he died a few years ago. I still visit his grave at Tideswell in Derbyshire and take flowers there every Armistice Day. He was a grand lad.

64.

Swede's Signalling Lesson

Jock Scurr – Private Signal Platoon

At 9 am on Tuesday 3 October 1950, 9 Platoon, C Company set out on a three-day operation in the Kulim triangle. I went as wireless-operator and took a new signaller, "Swede" Martin, with me to show him the job. This was the first duffy any of us had undertaken since we had returned to the mainland following our two months of Rest and Retraining in Penang. At the briefing the previous night, Second Lieutenant Wride, Platoon Commander, had announced that as we were all out of practice, we would have a rest at the top of each hill we climbed. This was very welcome news.

Our transport dropped us off at the fifth milestone on the eastern road of the triangle. We marched west and waded waist-deep across three sections of a winding river right at the start. After that, the country was nearly all rubber. We climbed some hills, finding it quite hard work, but the fact that Swede and I were able to take turns carrying the "68" set was a big help.

At the top of our fourth or fifth hill, we stopped for our fourth or fifth rest as promised. I lowered the set to the ground and flopped down. My body, shirt and slacks were drenched in sweat, I was breathing heavily and my heart was thumping for all it was worth. I glanced at Swede sitting beside me, whose chest was also visibly heaving. Swede came from somewhere near Yeovil in Somerset. He was about my medium height but of a stronger, thickset build.

"Fuck this for a lark, Jock!" he said now.

"It gets a lot worse," I told him, taking a small swig from my water-bottle. "It's worse in the jungle."

Then Swede said: "I be just thinking about when me and my mates went up to London on a railwaymen's outing. We went to the Windmill and saw all them naked women. We'd never seen anything like it! Even when we first went in and were going up the staircase, there were all these photographs on the walls of women, all starkers. We were all saying "Looks'ee 'ere! Looks'ee 'ere!" We just couldn't believe it!"

By now I had regained enough breath to be able to laugh freely. Swede was always making us laugh. It was the way he told them, as the saying goes.

Soon, we formed up and moved on. Eventually, we came to a deserted squatter area and made base in the Chinese smokehouse. I decided to set up the wireless on the verandah and stretch the aerial-wire from the rafters to a tree about twenty yards or so away. Proceeding to the tree, closely followed by Swede, I looked up at the branch about fifteen feet up that I wanted the wire to go across.

"D'you want me to climb up with it?" Swede offered.

"No," I said. "I don't bother with climbing trees. I always sling the aerial over like this." I quickly tied the end of the wire to the ring on the cross-guard of my bayonet and then threw the weapon skywards. To my chagrin, the bayonet bounced off some intervening foliage and fell back down, just missing my head. I then made two more attempts with the same result.

"I'd better climb up," I said now, red faced.

"D'you want me to climb up?" Swede offered again.

"No, it's OK," I replied a little edgily. Holding the end of the coiled wire, I shinned up the trunk rather slowly and awkwardly.

From below Swede commented: "You be making a right hash of that, Jock. You should have let me do it. I be a countryman. I be used to climbing trees."

"Is that a fact?" I called down, irritated: "Well, we have quite a few trees on the hills round Edinburgh!"

Reaching the branch, I passed the wire over it, but in the process I jolted against the adjacent foliage and was suddenly showered in red ants, most of which seemed to find their way beneath my shirt. As what felt like 100 pincers dug sharply and painfully into my flesh, I cried out: "Oh, bollocks!" Whereupon I lost my grip on the tree and toppled down, hitting the ground with a thud.

Swede was in stitches of laughter as he watched me rip open my shirt and frantically pound and swipe at the little red bastards that were mercilessly puncturing my chest and stomach.

"Shut up, you bloody Sassenach!" I protested.

Swede only laughed all the more. I thought he was never going to stop. When I had finally vanquished my assailants, I secured the end of the aerial-wire round the tree and then uncoiled the wire on the way back to the smokehouse verandah. I hastily explained to Swede that my bayonet-throwing system had always worked satisfactorily before, apart from one occasion during the Lenggong duffy when I had thrown my bayonet sheathed in its scabbard. Upon snagging in the fork of a branch, the scabbard had flown off and disappeared forever into a tangle of undergrowth!

After running the wire across an overhead beam and connecting it to the wireless, I obtained a SITREP (Situation Report) from Second Lieutenant Wride as the next Battalion transmission time approached.

Considering my rather poor performance in erecting the aerial, I was now anxious to demonstrate my ability as a wireless-operator to my pupil. I duly tuned in to the Battalion frequency, receiving Control's call-sign at strength three, rough-netted and then netted into Control's signal. So far so good! But when Control called for "Report of Signals", I was devastated to find that my reply was not received.

Desperately, during the hours that followed, I took the set to pieces three times, changed a valve and twice relocated the aerial (without mishap!) but it was all to no avail. I was unable to pass my message. In fact, I had no reason to reproach myself. Wireless contact in that kind of terrain was frequently just not possible, but I nonetheless felt rather guilty when I had to report to the Platoon Commander that I had been unable to get through.

First thing next morning however – lo and behold – Control received my signal and I was able to send the SITREP. After having explained to Swede the night before about mountain barriers to radio waves, skip distance, the ionosphere, etc, little of which I understood myself, I told him now that atmospheric conditions were invariably better in the morning, and I certainly felt that my credibility as an experienced signaller had to some extent been restored.

Before we continued on our way, Corporal Orum took his Sten gun and shot a mad, starving dog that had been left chained-up in one of the deserted bashas. If my luck hadn't changed that morning, I think I might have been tempted to ask him to put me out of my misery, as well!

65.

A Surprise Encounter

Charlie McAllister – Corporal C Company

While on patrol with 8 Platoon, looking for bandits' tracks or camps in the Kulim area late in 1950, we were moving along a track through the jungle when we came upon a clearing of tall grass with a hut on the far side. I halted the patrol and moved on ahead to check the area.

As I reached a crossing, I heard a rustling noise. I quickly raised my Owen gun ready to fire when the black snout, glowing eyes and striped, tawny hide of a full-grown tigress, accompanied by a cub, came face-to-face with me out of the undergrowth. I was so surprised, I turned and hastened back down the track as fast as I could, while the tigress retreated just as quickly back the way she had come, along with her offspring.

The rest of the patrol wondered what was happening when they saw me come flying down the track, but we all had a good laugh afterwards.

66.

Tubby's Bint

Ernie Stockton – Private HQ Company

In October 1950 when the Suffolks took over our barracks in Penang for a while, Battalion HQ moved to the old Jap airfield at Sungei Patani. One day, three of us from the MI Room decided to go down town. There was Jim Cornfield, "Tubby" Gleason and myself. Sungei Patani wasn't a big place but we went for a look round to see if there was anything worth buying and to try for a leg-over.

As we were strolling along a road, we saw this lovely Chinese bint. I always remember what a figure she had. You could tell she was on the game by the way she looked at us. So we spun a coin for first go. Tubby won, so he went off with her. The lucky sod! – or so we thought.

He hadn't been gone long when we heard him shouting: "Jim! Stocky!" So we ran down the street and into the house, thinking he was getting done-over. But it was OK. Apparently, he had just got ready to get his leg over and started to grope the bint when he found out it was a man dressed up! So we gave the sod a fucking good thumping and threw him in the river amongst all the shit and slime. But by now, all the rest of the people from the place were shouting and screaming at us, so we had to run like hell and get a taxi back to camp.

That was our first trip to Sungei Patani. We never went down again for about two weeks – and then we all got a bint.

67.

A Chilling Discovery

Frank Keenan – Lance Corporal C Company

In the Anak Kulim area in October 1950, 8 Platoon came upon a small bandit camp on a hill. Both parties were surprised; I don't know who recovered first. We were in single file with Ginger Thompson as leading scout, and only the guys at the front could fire. The bandits ran off and we went back down the hill.

Second Lieutenant Crisp told us that the bandits might come back for the arms we had found if they thought we had gone. So at dusk, we put ambushes back in the camp and across the track on the other hill with Platoon HQ in the basha at the top of the valley.

At the camp there were eight or ten men positioned in pairs. Late in the night, some bandits turned up and started tapping on the trees to try to draw the fire of the intended ambush. It worked. Two grenades were thrown by Corporal Hudspeth. I think they may have fallen close to where Hicks and Powell were and that's why they left their position. But how Hicks got separated from Powell I will never know. A bandit jumped on Hicks in the dark and tried to strangle him, but Hicks broke away and a lance corporal in the camp thought it was the bandits rushing them, so he opened fire, hitting Hicks fatally.

I was with the ambush party across the track on the other hill. Next to me was a Private Saunders who kept opening fire. When I asked him what he was firing at, he said he could see bandits down below, but I couldn't see them.

We all joined up again next morning. Joe Short, someone else and myself were sent up the hill to the camp to bring down Hicks' body. When we'd had breakfast, a party of us carried the body back to the road. There was Corporal Hudspeth, Joe Short, Parny Jones, some others and myself.

When we looked at Hicks' body on the main approach track, we discovered a bootlace tied tightly round his neck with a knot in it. That was when we began to realise that something had happened to Don Hicks before he was shot.

68.

Ambush or Kip?

Jock Scurr – Private Signal Platoon

On Monday morning 30 October 1950, half of 9 Platoon, C Company was briefed for a night ambush operation and I was detailed to go along as signaller. Very unusually, the patrol was to be commanded by CQMS Aird, a small, intelligent and kind-hearted NCO who was normally a base wallah. Aird had been assigned this task at his own request as he wished to experiment with individual 24-hour ration packs as a possible alternative to the normal communal cooking of compo rations. It was obvious to me from the start that Aird was very excited about his chance to lead a fighting patrol and was intent on making the best of this rare opportunity.

About twenty strong, we left Kulim camp at 1.30 pm in motor transport which eventually dropped us off amongst the rubber trees of Dublin Estate. From here we searched for a while along the edge of the Gunong Inas Forest Reserve, seeking a track that would lead us into the jungle in order to reach another specific track which bandits were reported to be regularly using. Our mission was to lay an ambush along this track that night.

After marching and counter-marching around the jungle edge for a couple of hours, we had failed to locate the appropriate approach track and halted for a much needed rest. CQMS Aird was squatted in the long grass amidst a group of old soldiers, studying his map and quite obviously feeling cheated by fate of his opportunity to prove his worth to the others in the Serjeants' Mess.

Eventually, Aird declared resolutely: "To hell with the track! I'm going to lay an ambush anyway."

The old soldiers around him exchanged alarmed and meaningful looks.

"What d'you mean?" asked Sandy Cooper, a Geordie who had

previously served in the Navy. "We haven't been able to find the track, so we'll just have to look for somewhere to kip down for the night."

"We could lay an ambush here," Aird pointed out.

"What? Here?" Sandy exclaimed, glancing concernedly at his two mates, Lightfoot and Clarke.

"Yes," said Aird. "After dark, the bandits might come along the edge of the jungle, right here."

"No, they wouldn't do that!" Sandy stated positively.

"How d'you know?" Aird persisted.

"Well -," Sandy hesitated, obviously unable to provide any reason why they wouldn't. "Look!" he now said in almost pleading tones. "You don't want to lay an ambush!"

Big Bob Lightfoot now lent his pal some support.

"We don't do things like that when we don't have to," he said. "You lie awake half the bloody night being eaten alive by leeches and mossies. Bollocks to that!"

"Well, I don't know," Aird said slowly, obviously starting to weaken.

Roy Clarke, a tall Canadian, now spoke. "I'm pretty sure there's a kampong back there where we can kip down in comfort," he drawled. "That's where I'd head for."

Roy was a former corporal who had reverted to the rank of private at his own request. Though a bit of a wild character at times, he was very intelligent and his opinion finally swayed CQMS Aird.

"OK," Aird said resignedly, "let's take a look."

The patrol now formed up in file and after we'd made a rather difficult crossing of a long stretch of paddy fields, we indeed came to a small Malay kampong. Here, the headman greeted us with great esteem and unceremoniously ordered a woman and her two children out of one of the raised up, wooden bashas in order to place this dwelling at our disposal. The woman, clutching her infants, came down the basha steps to seek accommodation for the night with a neighbour. She gave us a swift but resentful glance, and I didn't blame her!

By now we were all very hungry and ready for conner but when we delved into the contents of our individual 24-hour ration packs, we found that they contained hardly enough to constitute one decent meal. Even worse, we found that the foodstuffs were all full of weevils. Consequently, I lived on biscuits and peanuts for the two days and I expect the others did much the same. Thankfully, 24-hour ration packs were never again issued to us for operations.

When CQMS Aird gave me his SITREP (Situation Report) with the map reference of our location and NTR (nothing to report) for me to transmit by wireless to the Company base at Kulim, he said to me ruefully: "I'd really have liked to lay an ambush."

Aird was a first-rate human being and I felt sorry for him. But I made no comment. On my customary forays with 8 Platoon, I just wasn't used to the privates deciding that the patrol should have a comfortable kip instead of laying an ambush!

We all spent a comparatively cosy night, sleeping on the wooden floorboards of the basha. Outside, was placed one double-manned sentry post, which was something else I wasn't used to. In 8 Platoon we always did stag singly.

Next morning, with his enthusiasm no doubt revitalised by a good night's sleep, CQMS Aird announced that we were going to try to find the track that we were supposed to have ambushed the previous night. Locating the beginning of a track a short distance from the kampong, we set off into the jungle. For several hours we followed a number of

23. Private Jock Scurr at Kulim camp, about to depart on patrol with 9 Platoon, C Company on 30 October 1950.

adjoining tracks and some stretches of river on a rather haphazard course. We plodded through a lot of water and mud, collecting stacks of leeches, and eventually found ourselves hacking our way through dense thickets of attap and rattan with no tracks whatsoever.

CQMS Aird didn't have a clue where we were and neither did anyone else. We simply bashed on, sweating buckets, climbing the inevitable steep hill-slopes, ducking beneath branches and linea creepers and literally tumbling down the other sides of the hills in a state of near collapse. At one point, I threw my rifle down a slope in sheer exasperation and slid down on my back after it. Our situation seemed to grow more and more hopeless.

Then, a miracle happened. Just after 4 pm, we climbed down yet another slope through jagged thorn-scrub and found ourselves in a shallow river which ran, to our great surprise and joy, out of the jungle and into the rubber. As we staggered out into the open with our shirts ripped, our arms bleeding and our lungs gasping for breath, CQMS Aird commented: "How poor old Jock managed it with his wireless set, I do not know!"

Later I wrote in my journal: "I'm fucked if I know either! I was fucked but as usual kept going."

From here we marched on until we located the main path through Dublin Estate where we halted while CQMS Aird and the two scouts went ahead to bring our transport from the pre-arranged rendezvous point. Quite soon, a 15-cwt truck arrived and all twenty of us piled onto it, some sitting on the bonnet and others hanging on the back. An opportune bandit with a Bren gun could really have made a killing! Arriving at the main road, some of us transferred to the waiting 3-tonner and we then carried on back to the Company base at Kulim.

Corpulent and jocular Serjeant "Taggy" Bell came out to greet us as we jumped down from the trucks in the MT Park.

"How did you get on?" he asked CQMS Aird.

Before Aird could reply, Sandy Cooper cut in, commenting derisively: "He was going to lay an ambush."

"Silly old sod!" Taggy chided good-humouredly.

Aird shrugged. I had no doubt that he was still disappointed that he hadn't laid a night ambush and – who knows? – perhaps bagged a couple of bandits.

I shouldered my "68" set and walked on painfully tender feet towards

121

the Signals billet below the old planter's bungalow. Just then, I caught a glimpse of Second Lieutenant "Killer" Crisp of 8 Platoon heading towards the Officers' Mess. This prompted me to consider that if you had to do exhausting marches in the jungle, it made more sense to do them when questing for bandits than when on your way home from a good night's kip.

When I later tested my wireless to see how it had fared during it's rough trip that day, the only thing that registered on the meter was the battery-reading! As for myself, a delicious cold shower went a long way towards alleviating my weariness, although I probably wouldn't be completely back to normal until the following day.

69.

The Great Art Robbery

John Kitchen – Lance Corporal QM Staff

There used to be a picture of a scantily clad Chinese girl hanging on the wall in the Broadway Cafe in Penang. Butch Graham, the Battalion butcher, and Corporal Tanner of the QM Staff decided it would look well on the wall of their hut at Airfield Camp, Sungei Patani, where we were all temporarily accommodated with Tac HQ in October 1950.

On a subsequent visit to Penang, the pair of them dined at the Broadway with two accomplices, carefully choosing a table close to the location of the picture. They waited until both waitresses, Loh Tow and Emily, were in the kitchen towards the end of their meal. One of them then seized the picture from the wall and they hid it under the table while they paid for their meal.

As they walked out, the four kept close together with the picture in the middle of them and smuggled it down the stairs and into the street before it was missed. I am sure when the proprietors of the cafe found it was missing, it would not have taken a detective to guess which group removed it. But as the picture was not valuable and as the Broadway made a lot of money out of customers from the KOYLI, no complaint was ever made.

24. (Left to right) Corporal Tanner, Private "Chopper" Easton and Lance Corporal "Butch" Graham of the QM Staff, three of the four culprits, with their ill-gotten "work of art". Sungei Patani, October 1950.

70.

Like It Was Yesterday

Frank Keenan – Lance Corporal C Company

On 23 November 1950, 8 Platoon fought an action near Junjong under the command of Second Lieutenant Crisp. It has all come back to me like it was only yesterday.

It all started the day before. We stopped late in the day at a deserted rubber tapper's basha where we ate. Then, Mr Crisp took us on an ambush, leaving Corporal McAllister, Freddy Mains and someone else guarding the basha and our equipment. At dusk, we were in the worst ambush position I ever saw. We had walked along this track for miles and couldn't find a good one. So we settled for this bend in the track, with some men above the track and myself and three others below.

We had just settled down when this Geordie said the bandits were coming. Mr Crisp said to hold our fire. However, just as the bandits got to this big rock jutting out onto the track, the Geordie lost his nerve and opened fire – for which I was truly thankful! The bandits now turned and scurried up above us in the rubber; then fired down on us. Someone else and myself opened fire up at the muzzle-flashes in the trees. At this point, the Civil Liaison Officer jumped up in front of me across the track and I almost hit him with a burst.

Mr Crisp then said: "That's it. The ambush is ruined." So we made our way back to the basha. As we arrived, Freddy Mains challenged

25. Frank Keenan of 8 Platoon, C Company, enjoying a mess-tin of "all in" stew at an operational base in the jungle.

us and then told Mr Crisp that after they had heard the shooting, they took up defensive positions and down the track had come this Chinese guy, running and out of breath. During the night, Mr Crisp and the CLO interrogated the Chinaman – you know what I mean – and the two of them and Stan Swalwell and myself took turns guarding him.

Now the next morning, after a hasty breakfast, a small patrol of us set out along the track with the Dyak and Mr Crisp leading. We had been on the move about half an hour when the track left the rubber and continued into jungle.

Then the shooting started and we all hit the deck except for Mr Crisp, who was the only one who knew what was happening. He remained standing and was shooting back at the bandit sentries with his carbine when the bottom of the magazine fell off and all the ammo spilled out. I had been bringing up the rear and when the shooting stopped, I asked the three people in front of me: "Where's Mr Crisp?"

They said he had gone on, so I took the lead and followed on down the hill. However, we missed Mr Crisp's direction and ran bang into a large group of bandits going round a bend in the track. We hit the deck again and I threw a grenade but forgot to pull the pin! Even so, the bandits made a run for it. They must have thought we were a much bigger party than we were.

I then heard renewed firing above to our left, so I led the men with me back up the track and found Mr Crisp with the Dyak, the CLO, Stan Swalwell and the Bren-gunner who we used to call "the bible-thumper". They were behind this large fallen tree, firing downhill. Mr Crisp then said: "Good, Corporal Keenan! I'm glad you're here!" and pointed to where a wounded bandit lay below.

The Dyak pulled my sleeve and pointed to all these bandits running across some open ground, trying to reach the jungle at the other side. It must have been the same group I'd run into down the hill. I opened fire along with the rest. The Dyak had a rifle but most of us had sub-machine-guns. Although my Owen gun didn't have the range, it felt good firing it. I may or may not have hit a few of the bandits – I couldn't say for sure – or some of the others may have hit some of them.

At this point, some bandits who Mr Crisp had pinned down were trying to get to the one who was shot in order to carry him away. So Mr Crisp put the Bren gun resting on the bible-thumper's shoulders and fired rapid bursts to keep them away from him. The hot cases were going down the bible-thumper's back as Mr Crisp kept firing. Finally, all the bandits took off and everything was quiet.

Mr Crisp then took my Owen gun and five of my mags and left me his pistol. His orders were that the Bren-gunner, the Dyak and myself should give him cover while he led the rest of the patrol down the hill to check the area. Mr Crisp then finished off the bandit on the ground by shooting him in and around the groin. He put a full mag of thirty rounds into him from my Owen gun. I can't think whether Freddy Mains also fired into him or not, but the bandit's body was like jelly after that. Mr Crisp then called me and my group down. We found clothing and equipment of other bandits scattered around, soaked in blood. The others must have taken the wounded ones away.

We ate tiffen with Freddy Mains sitting on the dead bandit. We then tied the body to a long branch and carried it to the road to board our transport back to Kulim.

71.

Sad Day at Serdang

Derek Ashley – Private MT Platoon

One of the incidents which has always stuck in my mind happened while I was with A Company at Serdang in December 1950. Some of the lads went off playing football and as always, they all had to carry a rifle and fifty rounds of ammunition each, as did the lads who went along as escorts. Well, when they came back to camp, it was raining cats and dogs. And how it could rain out there! So, on getting off the trucks, everyone dashed back to their tents without lining up for the usual – "Unload. For inspection, port arms".

After only a short while, I was in the MT tent with the other drivers when we heard such a loud bang – it was like a grenade going off. Later, we learned that one of the lads who had been playing football had been accidentally shot by another lad in his own tent. The casualty died in the ambulance on the way to the MRS in Kulim, and the next day I had to take his body to Taiping in my truck for a military funeral.

The deceased was a fellow named Gregory who came from Oswestry in Shropshire. The poor lad who shot him was terribly distressed. He came from somewhere in Herefordshire. General Sibbald (a lieutenant in 1950) told me at a Reunion in Doncaster that Gregory had been the first casualty under his command in his army career.

On a more cheerful note, I have always remembered when I had to transport fresh rations to the rifle companies for Charlie, the civilian contractor, when his truck broke down. The first thing I had to do was go to an ice factory and pick up three one-ton blocks of ice. You would think these would melt in the heat but they didn't. When we arrived at the companies, the ice was broken up with a hammer and put in galvanised baths. I did this run together with some of the other drivers for quite a while.

72.

Finger in the Pie

Jock Scurr – Private Signal Platoon

There was a clerk in HQ Company whom I shall call John. One evening, John went to the AKC (Army Kinema Corporation) cinema in Minden (formerly Glugor) Barracks, Penang. Hardly had he taken his seat when the wife of an absent soldier sat down in the seat next to him. After only a few minutes this lady – whom I shall call Mrs Mulvaney – reached over and grasped John's hand which she then guided beneath her dress and up the inside of her bare thigh. Rather alarmed, John now endeavoured to withdraw his hand but Mrs Mulvaney firmly seized hold of it and poked herself with his middle finger very vigorously over a considerable period of time, accompanied by a noticeable change in her breathing pattern.

John later told me: "I've always been a gentlemanly type who is prepared to oblige a lady in any way I can but I really thought this was a bit much, as the RSM was sitting directly in front of me and I was finding it very hard to concentrate on the film!"

Some weeks following this incident, one of the attached personnel – whom I shall call Joe – found himself as escort to women from the

127

"Married Families" on their weekly shopping trip into Georgetown. Seated beside Mrs Mulvaney in the back of the vehicle, Joe also found that his hand was greatly appreciated beneath her dress; only being a dirty bastard, he made the most of it!

That night, knowing that the lady's husband was away on the mainland and having no doubt that he was on a definite cert, Joe made a stealthy midnight visit to the Married Quarters and with considerable agility climbed up to Mrs Mulvaney's balcony. At that moment, however, Mrs Mulvaney awoke from her slumbers and perceiving a dark figure on the point of climbing through her bedroom window, she proceeded to scream her head off. Joe now had no choice but to leap back down from the balcony and run for his life.

Despite the fright that Mrs Mulvaney had received, it apparently did not alter her practice of groping any male who might find himself beside her in the back of a 15-cwt truck whilst on the way into town to attend Mass on a Sunday morning!

73.

Small Gains

Gordon Hill – Lance Corporal B Company

When we were stationed at Kroh in December 1950, we received a report that Communists were being supplied with food and clothing from a nearby squatter area. Moved in from the rear through the jungle, 6 Platoon took up position along the back of the squatter area. At the same time, the Marines were called up to come in from the road and advance through the area to drive any Communists towards us.

To our surprise, the Marines turned up in full dress rather than jungle kit. With their brasses glinting in the sun, they could have been picked off a mile away! No bandits appeared but when we searched the bashas in the area, we found a Communist flag and a girl making uniforms. The police were duly called and the girl was taken away to be interrogated.

Six months later, in June 1951, I was sent with four men on a patrol in the Junon region. We passed through a Chinese squatter area near to the road and continued towards a kampong from where we heard gunfire. We approached with caution but soon realised it was the kampong guards firing at some monkeys. So we passed through the kampong and on into the jungle to cut back to the road.

Approaching the road, we spotted a look-out post in a tree which had been used for monitoring police and military movement on the road. We destroyed this post and made a report which led to another patrol being sent out.

Numerous small gains like these helped to finally defeat the enemy in Malaya.

74.

A Cobbler's Story

John Kitchen – Lance Corporal QM Staff

Among the attached personnel in HQ Company was Jock Gribbin, a Glaswegian lance corporal of the RAOC who was employed as the Battalion cobbler. Jock had a cobbler's shop at the far end of Minden Barracks in a very quiet location, well away from the other stores controlled by the Quartermaster.

Having become very friendly with some of the laundresses from Mr Shamshudin's dhobi and not being a person to miss any tricks, Jock told several of his friends that he could fix them up with a "bint". At the same time, he offered them the facilities of the cobbler's shop to have their wicked ways with the ladies of their choice from amongst several beauties at a price payable to him, which he would use to pay for services rendered, less a "small" commission.

From the first day this venture was not a great success, as the "beauties" turned out to be only one very plump, older lady who even the most frustrated, lovelorn young soldiers were not prepared to pay for. The consensus of opinion was that they'd rather have a Tiger beer at the NAAFI. So Jock's mini-brothel closed down before he got it started.

75.

Ambush With a Difference

Bill Lyness – Corporal B Company

At the end of 1950, 6 Platoon was stationed at Klian Intan near the Thailand border. Acting on so-called information about bandit movement in the area, a patrol of eight men was sent out on a one-night ambush. Second Lieutenant Harrison was in command with myself, a corporal at the time, Number Two.

We left camp in a truck at about 2 pm and drove for an hour in the direction of the Thai border. We then stopped at the side of the road by a railway line. It was intended that the patrol should walk up the railway line to a spot marked on the map and stay in ambush for the night. After walking for about one hour, we stopped for a rest and a brew-up. We then set off again until we came to a track crossing the railway line. This was the point on the map that we were to ambush, according to Second Lieutenant Harrison.

Investigation of the ambush site revealed that the track split into two parts, leading off separately into the thick bush. So it was decided that I would take three men to ambush the left-hand fork and Mr Harrison would take the other three along the fork to the right. By this time it was getting dark. I led my men a short way down our track, picked a good spot with some cover and got everyone into position for the ambush. I then put three men on watch and one man resting and every two hours swopped one man over, giving each man a rest and a little sleep.

This worked very well until about 6 am when I was the one who was resting. It was just breaking dawn when one of the lads came to me and said he thought he had seen someone in the bush about 100 yards down the track. As this was a curfew area, no one should have been about at that time. So I said: "If anyone comes down the track, shoot them."

I was just pulling my boots on when the Bren gun opened fire. This lasted for only a few minutes; then there was complete silence. On investigation, it was found that two Malays had been shot, one fatally and the other one wounded. Both men were lying by the track and were armed with rifles. At first, this seemed to be a good result but on closer inspection in the cold light of dawn, we realised that both Malays were kampong guards – trained and armed by the Malay Police to defend their village against the bandits.

We applied first aid to the wounded man's leg and carried him down the track to the kampong. By this time the natives were getting a bit restless, so we quickly packed our kit and made a beeline for the road. Second Lieutenant Harrison informed the police as soon as possible about our terrible mistake and apologised for the error.

The end product came about two months later when Second Lieutenant Harrison and I went up to Alor Star to attend an Inquiry about the incident. All the way up there, Mr Harrison kept saying: "Don't forget you shouted halt three times." That was a laugh! No chance! But the Inquiry accepted our explanation and nothing more was said.

It seemed that somewhere along the line we had got the map reference wrong and were in the wrong place – which wasn't at all unusual.

76.

A Warning Unheeded

Gordon Hill – Lance Corporal B Company

In the Kroh area late in 1950, it was planned that 6 Platoon would lay an ambush outside a kampong, so the kampong guards were warned in advance.

On the night of the ambush, two of the guards did not heed our warning and ran across the clearing where the ambush was laid. The Bren-gunner opened fire, hitting one of the guards, and the other guard then called out who they were. So the Platoon Commander, the Junior Civil Liaison Officer and two scouts went over to see what had happened. They found the guard lying on the ground and when his sarong was lifted up, it was discovered that he had been hit in his private parts and was bleeding badly.

Not much could be done for the bleeding but the officer injected him with morphine. We then made a makeshift stretcher, called off the ambush and proceeded with the wounded kampong guard about five miles down a railway track to the nearest station. But the guard was dead on arrival. The JCLO tried to arouse the stationmaster but as he was speaking in Chinese, the stationmaster thought we were Communists and wouldn't open up. However, he finally did open the door and phoned for an ambulance.

The Bren-gunner later had to appear at a Court of Inquiry but was excused, considering it had not been his fault.

77.

Jungle Hats and Rifles

Jock Scurr – Private Signal Platoon

There was something about a jungle hat. Apart from his rifle (or other personal weapon) a soldier could grow more attached to his jungle hat than to any other item of equipment. Ripped shirts and slacks and rotted socks and jungle boots had to be periodically replaced but only rarely would a soldier trade in his jungle hat for renewal.

When first issued, of course, a jungle hat was nothing special – just a circular crown of green cloth with a floppy brim. But with careful shaping, wiring, sewing and attachment of various adornments, the hat could be completely transformed into an extension of the wearer's personality.

Some flamboyant characters managed to obtain hats with especially wide brims and completed the cowboy appearance with a long loop of cord which was tightened or slackened beneath the chin by means of a bead runner. Others wore either a plain or plaited cord which passed over the crown and held up the brim at the sides. Hats were perched and brims bent at every angle; some with the brim up at the back and down at the front, some with the brim up either at one side or both sides, while down-to-earth, no-nonsense types wore their hats square on their heads with the brims pulled resolutely down all round.

I loved my jungle hat. I sewed a few stitches round the ridge of the crown to keep it from sagging and attached a shoelace which could pass round my chin to keep the hat secure on my head when travelling in the back of a fast-moving truck or when marching through areas of jungle where the jagged thorns of trailing vines regularly whisked the hat from your head. Most of the time, though, I wore the lace across the front of the brim, which jointly held the front down and the edges of the sides bent up, thus achieving my chosen design. There was one man I knew who had the temerity to believe that he had the best hat in the Company. I knew that this could not possibly be true. When I looked in the mirror, I was convinced that there was no contest.

After a year and a half of jungle-bashing, my hat became battered and faded – rather like myself – but when it was time to go home, I just could not bear to part with it. I obtained another hat from my cousin that I was able to hand into the stores with the rest of my jungle kit and consequently brought my cherished jungle hat home to Blighty in my kitbag.

As for personal weapons: In 8 Platoon, Matt Busby regularly used to pat his Bren gun and call it "a good boy", while leading scout Ginger Thompson named his Sten gun "Betsy". When later Ginger reluctantly, though advisedly, traded Betsy in for a more accurate and reliable Owen gun, his new "friend" became "Betsy Number Two".

For myself, there was no weapon like a rifle. I'd always been attracted to bolt-action rifles ever since I'd watched Gary Cooper using one with deadly effect against attacking Tuareg tribesmen in the film *Beau Geste*. And in the Army Cadets I had been greatly impressed by the accuracy and hard-hitting power of the old SMLE Mark III. The type of rifle that we used in Malaya was a . 303 Lee-Enfield No. 5 which weighed nine pounds and was consequently two pounds lighter than the No. 4 standard issue and had a shorter barrel with a flash eliminator; all of which made the No. 5 very suitable for jungle operations.

What pleased me most about my rifle was the feeling of strength and security that it gave me. On operations, I was always reassured by the knowledge that I had in my hands the means of inflicting considerable damage upon any adversary who might threaten me.

My rifle and I eventually reached the parting of the ways but I still retain my jungle hat to this day.

78.

Christmas at the Broadway

Roy Caldecott – Lance Corporal A Company

During my time on the mainland jungle-bashing with A Company at Grik, Kroh, Sungei Patani and elsewhere, sometimes I didn't know myself. Can someone help? A semblance of sanity returned when, through weekend soccer or on Company rests and refits, I made my many visits to Penang.

As the months of 1950 rolled by, I took advantage of one such occasion to visit the Bazaar where I knew there was a good antique stall somewhere at the back. Locating the stall, I searched through the ramshackle bits and pieces until I found what I was looking for. I had spotted it several weeks before.

"What is it for?" the stall-holder asked.

"A Christmas present," I replied.

"You're a little early."

"Better now than never. How much?"

"Fifteen dollars."

"Polish it up and I'll give you twelve."

"Done."

We shook hands. I had purchased an old silver snuffbox with a snap-shut lid and a small two-inch chain. I had thought it would look nice on Maureen's "slave chain".

In the meantime, Maureen had taken charge of our tickets for a free Christmas dinner at the Broadway which she had so craftily obtained with the aid of a dead wasp. She had full control of the arrangements and, of course, her sister Hazel had to help. In her correspondence, Maureen had told me that the manager couldn't reserve a cubicle for either Christmas Eve or Christmas Day, so he had reserved one for Boxing Day. No matter, I thought. We fortunately had an important game on Boxing Day, so I knew there would be no difficulty of me not being on the island.

The day eventually came. I couldn't wait for the final whistle to blow. Then, off I went. I arrived at the Broadway early, around 5.30 pm give or take a few minutes. The idea was to get a couple of brandies down before 6 pm; the time we were all to meet. I checked the cubicle with the manager. All seemed OK, so I slipped him a five-dollar note and settled down at a table in the main room to have my drinks.

Unseen by me from where I was sitting, Maureen arrived at 5.45, so I had no chance to have my two brandy glasses removed. She twisted my ear from behind. "And what are you doing here early?" she enquired.

"I just thought I would," I said lamely.

"Never mind you just thought!" She broke off from what she was saying and I was glad. Opening her shoulder-bag, she placed two packages on the table and said: "Just you think of what you have to do later."

"You think of everything," I said, standing up and giving her a kiss on her cheek – a very unusual thing for her to allow me to do in a public place.

The next to arrive were Hazel and her boyfriend Paul. As we all shook hands, I noticed that two strangers had closely followed them up the stairs. I was now introduced to another police officer, a little taller than Paul but also a very handsome Malay.

"This is Peter," Paul told me. "And his fiancée, Soo."

Again there were handshakes all round. Soo was Chinese and a real beauty. Let me now tell you what the ladies were wearing. All wore silk cheongsams; Maureen in pale blue, Hazel in scarlet and Soo in white. Maureen wore her slave chain in the higher position which really stood out through the silk. Hazel's dress, I remember, had a golden fleck woven into it and Soo's dress was just like nacre, and what a pearl it covered! As my eyes appreciated this, I felt Maureen's heel pressing down on my toes. I gave her a guilty glance and was relieved that she winked at me.

The manager now came to usher us to our cubicle. The usual table had been removed and replaced with a larger, oval one with six chairs. We all sat down; three on either side, each facing his or her partner. Having taken the snuffbox from my pocket, I handed it to Maureen. "Merry Christmas," I said.

"What is it?" she asked.

"It's an old silver snuffbox for you to put on your chain." I pointed and placed my finger on the heart-shaped medallion covering her navel beneath the silk.

"I don't take snuff," she said, screwing up her nose.

"OK then," I said. "You can always put a dead wasp into it."

She laughed and in their own tongue she explained to the others what had happened that night almost a year before. Maureen was enjoying her story but I was a little concerned that Paul and Peter might take a professional interest in such a dodge. However, one of them remarked flippantly that such things could happen in the best of circles. So I left it at that.

Our first course was a clear Chinese soup with the usual roll and knob of butter. As required, we helped ourselves to more from the large bowl left in the centre of the table. The next course was a serving of oysters.

"How many?" the waitress enquired.

"How do they come?" I asked.

"By the dozen," Hazel said from my left.

"By the dozen?" I hesitated.

"Yes, please," said Paul and Peter.

They had a dozen each. The ladies had six, so I had six and received a smile from Paul and Peter and a "tut-tut" from Maureen. A bottle of champagne accompanied the oysters.

The main course came. Maureen knew how I was with chopsticks; I had made a fool of myself before. Two waitresses brought in a large silver platter on which was a large silver bowl. Two more silver platters were placed one at each end of the table. The manager approached Maureen and asked who was to have the special. She nodded her head towards me opposite. From the large, steaming bowl the two platters were loaded with prawns, chicken and raw fish of many varieties. It was what, I have learned since, was called "a Steamboat". The Steamboat now being in place and my companions choosing with their chopsticks whatever took their fancy through openings around the bowl, the manager again arrived.

He placed a large, oval plate before me and removed the cover, and there was the biggest steak I had ever seen. Not only was it accompanied by the usual vegetables, which Maureen inspected with one of her chopsticks, there were king prawns, liver and chips. Also supplied was a knife and fork. Orders came from across the table: "Let me see how good you are with that." This brought smiles from the others and there were even broader grins when half-way through I stood up to loosen my belt.

By now the champagne was taking effect and we were reaching a stage when our minds were growing a little frivolous. I told them the story of the National Service lad and the coconut matting, to which Soo commented from my right that someone must have been a learner. A cough came from Peter behind his hand. Peter was normally stationed at Pekan, way down on the east coast. He was with the Ocean Police. Recently he had made an important arrest; not only seizing several tons of opium, some raw, some slightly treated, but the big catch was a wanted baron who had a price on his head. For this he had been promoted, he told us, tapping his second pip. In response to a signal

26. Roy Caldecott in 1950, wearing a tie Maureen had given him for a birthday present. Behind him are Private Eric Barratt (left) and Lance Corporal Dave Sinclair, also of A Company.

he had given, the waitress now came in with a larger bottle of champagne. "My contribution," he said, which we all applauded.

For his part, Paul had for some time now been stationed with other constabulary at the Burma Triangle. For good work there he too had obtained his second pip.

Everyone was now getting a little merry. I was surprised at Maureen. It was the first time I had seen her drink anything stronger than cream soda; but then again, she was among her own people and it was a celebration. The waitress came in again at about 10 pm. This time she brought in a little Chinese tea bowl and a pot of boiling water. Orders again came from over the table: "If you have to get back at midnight, it is getting nearly time."

I broke open one of the packages and poured the contents into the bowl.

"This time, the two," Maureen said.

The contents of the second package went into the bowl. Maureen then lifted the bowl, took the lid off the teapot, and into the pot went the contents of both packages. After giving the brew a good stir, she replaced the lid and filled the bowl with some of the brew. I sat with one hand on each side of the bowl, waiting for it to cool. Hazel placed one hand on top of mine from her side and Soo did the same from the other. I looked across at Maureen. She winked at me and I drank the bowl of brew.

"You'll be fine tonight," Hazel said softly.

"You're a lucky boy," Soo added.

Maureen was standing now. She held out her hand to me. I clasped it and we left, uttering warm but brief goodbyes. We only had eyes for each other.

That night was exceptional. As Soo had said, I was truly a lucky boy.

79.

A Handful of Death

Gordon Hill – Lance Corporal B Company

Having set off from our base at Pelam Estate on 26 January 1951, the MT dropped us off a few miles down the main track. From here we proceeded into the rubber with 4 Platoon leading. Jimmy Whitehead was one of their scouts. We patrolled for a few miles and then had a break.

After the break, it was 6 Platoon's turn to take the lead. In charge were Second Lieutenant Harrison and Serjeant Sanders. The leading scout was myself, Lance Corporal Gordon Hill and the second scout was Private Arthur Bills. As I went up front to take the lead, I passed Jimmy who was sitting at the side of the track. He had emptied his magazine and holding out the bullets in his hand, he said to me: "Look, Gord, a handful of death." That was the last time I saw him before he was struck down by a Communist bullet.

We were now in the jungle and carried on chopping our way through until we came to an area where some trees had been cut down. There was no one there but tools were lying on the ground. We continued along the edge of the clearing and came across a track that ended abruptly, which indicated that it had been used by the Communists. One of their tricks was to go in different directions to break the track so as not to give their position away. On the ground here was a fountain pen which made Arthur Bills and myself suspicious. We summoned Second Lieutenant Harrison and showed it to him but he ordered us to carry on through the rest of the jungle, turn down the hill and cut across the bottom.

It was after 6 Platoon had reached the bottom with 4 Platoon following, when Major Sutcliffe, the Company Commander, spotted the Communists at the top of the hill. He shouted an order and launched an assault up the slope. This was difficult, as by now we were back among rubber trees where the ground was a type of red ash which fell away under our feet as we tried to advance.

139

We hastened to get to cover as the Communists opened fire. We then saw Jimmy fall and realised he had been hit. We returned the fire and continued up the hill. One of our EY riflemen fired a grenade which hit a tree and exploded above us, showering us with shrapnel. One man was injured in the foot. Arthur Bills and myself moved up one side to try to cut off the enemy's escape but they must have fled out the other side into the jungle. We carried on and found that there must have been a rearguard left at the jungle side, as they kept firing at us. At this time, Judo Roberts and Serjeant Dee shot and killed one of the Communists who was later revealed to be an officer.

We now returned to where Jimmy had been shot. We found he had been shot through the mouth and was dead. Corporal Billy Lyness was

27. Lance Corporal Jim Whitehead (left) of B Company, just a month before his death. He is seen here with Private A Lowden in December 1950.

standing over him and had placed his hat over his face. I was told Jimmy would have been going home a month later.

Regrouped, 6 platoon gave chase, but to no avail, while 4 platoon stayed behind to send off a message and to search the camp.

A few days later, 6 Platoon was patrolling in the same area when we came upon a clearing in the jungle which was very swampy. There were four recently killed Communists in the swamp which we believed could have been put there after the skirmish in which Jimmy Whitehead was killed. Not being definitely able to take credit for this, we sent for the police to remove the bodies. The police came with makeshift stretchers and, with bandannas over their noses and mouths to reduce the smell, they carried the bodies to nearby waiting vehicles and took them away for identification.

Only a couple of days or so after that, 6 Platoon was called out to deal with an incident in the Junon area between Malays and Chinese after the Malays had found out that the Chinese in a local village were supplying food to the Communists. We found an old man with his face slashed and those killed included children. The head of a small child was found in a basket. Pigs and other animals were tied up and the village had been set on fire. There were pigs running around with half of their bodies burned. The smell was terrible.

It took us a few days to sort it all out, and we were very glad when we could finally return to the Company base.

80.

Premonition?

Gerry Sweeney – Private B Company

I first met Jim Whitehead in October 1946 at Magdalene Fields Camp, Berwick-upon-Tweed. He was a big, six-foot ex-miner from Grimethorpe, Barnsley, with a ready laugh and some droll sayings. From Berwick we moved to the newly formed Light Infantry Training Camp at Farnborough and after completion of training in early 1947, we went our separate ways. Jim was posted to the 1st Battalion at Minden, Germany, and I joined the 2nd Battalion at Deolali, India.

We next met up in Penang. He had come out to Malaya and gone to A Company. I was in B Company and as it happened, both companies were in Glugor Barracks at the same time for a few days rest. Then, in October 1950 Jim was transferred to B Company, so we were teamed up again in 6 Platoon.

In January 1951 we were stationed on a rubber plantation at Lubok Segintah, just a few miles from Sungei Patani. On the 26th of that month, we were due to go out on a patrol but it was just a one-day job; no sweat, as we used to say. We were woken quite early as we had to be at the dropping-off point for first light.

Just as we were ready to leave our tents, I noticed Jim was strangely quiet. We had managed to have a few bottles of Tiger the previous night, so I said to him: "Are we fit, then?"

Instead of the usual laugh and daft remark about the purpose of the

28. An earlier photo of Jim Whitehead (right) when he was serving with A Company. With him are Lance Corporal Paxton and Private Potts.

patrol, Jim just turned to me and said: "No. I am bloody fed up with this game ! I'll be glad to get on the boat home." He had never in all the time I had known him looked and sounded so down in the mouth. Even Bill Lyness, our other mate, could not cheer him up.

I remember shortly before the previous Christmas, we were at Kroh and had just returned to camp from a pretty gruelling three-to-four days patrol, when our Platoon Commander realised he had left his compass at one of our halts during that last day's march. After a confab between him and the Company Commander, he came to us and said: "Lyness, Sweeney and Whitehead, we are going to drop you off in the morning to retrace the route and recover the compass."

Whereupon Jim turned and said to us in a loud whisper: "He thinks we are fucking immortal!" In the event, common sense prevailed and the compass was written off. But that was Jim; no moaning and groaning – just a droll remark for the officer's benefit.

So, on 26 January 1951 we set out on patrol and everything was going quite well. We were in secondary jungle and making good progress when suddenly we came under fire from above. I was in the scout group at the front of the patrol and Jim was with the centre party. Myself and Corporal "Lofty" Watts managed to get around the base of the hill and made our way steadily up the flank where the fire wasn't so heavy. As we were approaching the crest, the firing stopped just as suddenly as it had started. It was typical guerrilla tactics – open up with heavy fire and then withdraw as quickly as possible into the jungle.

As Lofty and I made our way to the centre of the hill, one of the lads said: "Hey Gerry, your mate's been hit."

I went round just below the crest and found Jim lying on his back. I could not see a mark on him, so I took my pack off to put beneath his head, saying: "You'll be all right, Jim. We'll soon get you fixed up." But then when I put my hand under his head, I realised that part of the back of his head had been blown away. The bullet must have entered his mouth and gone straight through. At least death would have been instantaneous.

My last memory of Jim was a tattoo he had on his chest which was now visible, as I had opened his shirt to look for a wound. The tattoo consisted of the KOYLI badge with the regimental motto *CEDE NULLIS* underneath, and below that in bold letters were the words BASH ON REGARDLESS – a very fitting epitaph for a first-class soldier. I still wonder to this day if his mood that morning was some kind of premonition of his impending death.

Jim was buried in Penang cemetery. Tom Morgan, a pal of his from A Company, has visited the grave in recent years and placed flowers upon it. He was also kind enough to send me a photograph of the grave.

It has also occurred to me how strange it was that just a few weeks prior to his death, Jim should have made the remark: "He thinks we are fucking immortal!"

81.

A Slightly Intolerant Act

John Kitchen – Lance Corporal QM Staff

Occasionally on Saturdays I used to go into Georgetown, Penang, with Lance Corporal Jock Gribbin, RAOC, the Battalion cobbler, usually for a meal and a movie. After dinner at the Broadway Cafe on one such evening, Jock suggested we should try out the City Lights dance hall. I had never been before, so I agreed and we subsequently took a trishaw.

We stopped about 150 yards from the dance hall and the trishaw wallah said he wanted to drop us off here as there was a queue of prospective patrons at a trishaw rank fifty yards in the other direction. When he adamantly declined to alter this decision, Jock, as a good Glasgow Scot, refused to pay. As we got out, the trishaw wallah began to curse us off and started screaming gibberish to the high heavens. Jock was not prepared to tolerate this behaviour. He tipped the trishaw up from the side we were on and promptly threw the trishaw and the operator into a monsoon ditch which was conveniently located on the other side.

We now took off in the direction of the City Lights, but after the trishaw wallah had climbed out of the ditch, he enlisted the assistance of a number of his brethren from the trishaw rank who all set out in pursuit. But as we had a good lead on our pursuers, we managed to slip quietly into the City Lights without incident and retired to the men's room for about fifteen minutes.

When we returned to the dance floor, we bought our dance tickets, chose our partners from among the hostesses and began to dance – not only to the music of the band but to the noise of a near riot outside. It seemed our pursuers were after the blood of any British soldiers in the hall, as they would have been hard pressed to identify the true culprits.

The management of the City Lights held the riotous crowd at bay outside and phoned Minden Barracks to send transport to take all the soldiers back to camp. When the truck appeared at the back entrance, we were all quietly loaded and returned to barracks. Strangely enough, no questions were asked; but if we had been questioned, neither Jock nor I would have admitted to that slightly intolerant act!

82.

Two and Two

Jock Scurr – Private Signal Platoon

In the opening month of 1951, I was sent on detachment with 9 Platoon, C Company to a rather dismal camp at Serdang. From here on the afternoon of Sunday 28 January, we set out to act on information that had been received by the Police. A Malay civilian was going to guide us to a spot in Sungei Siputeh Estate where it was reported that bandits had been seen digging trenches. The quickest way into the area was via Junjong, but we drove a fair distance past this Communist den so that none of the inhabitants might suspect our destination and possibly send out a warning to their uniformed comrades.

After eventually debusing, we then made our way on foot back through the rubber. Suddenly, the heavens opened up and we were rapidly soaked to the skin and then drenched even more thoroughly as we crossed a long stretch of open paddy fields. As we neared the end of the paddy, we warily eyed a nearby, massive "shit-buffalo" that bucked and reared it's horned head menacingly. After that, we waded a knee-deep river and after a short rest, continued to some deserted wooden bashas where Second Lieutenant David Wride decided to make our base.

From here Number One Section, reinforced by the Bren-gunner and two Sten-gunners from Number Two Section, plus myself (minus my wireless set) continued on our mission. After about half an hour of a fairly swift march through overgrown rubber trees, the Malay guide halted at the foot of a hill and pointed nervously up to the ridge.

Cautiously we began to climb, maintaining normal patrol formation in file. When about half-way up the hill, we halted and spread out into extended order. Then Mr Wride gave the signal to advance and with weapons at the ready and trying as best we could to keep our line, we continued to climb. The bushy slope was steep and hard going but we nonetheless moved at a fair speed. With fingers on triggers and feeling "all-in", we finally scrambled to the top. But there were no signs of any bandits or fortifications. We searched around the ridge amongst the thick ferns and undergrowth but all we found was a months-old structure of a basha.

The guide now led us to another hill, then another, both of which we searched without any success. It was growing pretty late, so Mr Wride decided we should call it a day and return to base. On our way back, we came to a lone, isolated basha from the door of which emerged nine young women whose ages ranged perhaps from 16 to 30. They stood watching us file by as though we were the most fascinating sight they had seen in ages. Needless to say, there were various ribald comments made by some of the lads regarding all manner of desired pleasurable activities, and the women, not understanding the actual words but no doubt getting a pretty clear picture, showed no sign of being offended and some of them responded with smiles.

It now began to pour with rain once more and we consequently arrived back at our base at the deserted bashas absolutely drenched. After a hot meal of canned steak and kidney pudding, we split up into two groups to spend the night in two of the bashas.

Mr Wride had given me a SITREP to transmit but I couldn't get my "68" set to even rough net, never mind net, so had to give up. Night was then rapidly descending and Mr Wride, crouching beside me before the wireless set, suddenly said to me in quiet and rather mysterious tones: "There were nine women and no men living in that basha we passed. D'you know what I think?" He paused dramatically and I shook my head. He then continued: "I think it's a bandit brothel!"

"A bandit brothel?" I started to laugh.

"I'm sure it is," Mr Wride stated emphatically. "I'm going back there tonight to ambush it. I'll take Steve with me, seeing he knows the local languages."

Steve was our Tamil Civil Liaison Officer.

"Well, I'll come with you," I said now eagerly.

"No, no," Mr Wride replied hastily. "The fewer people the better on this kind of a job. Far less likelihood of being detected."

And far more likelihood of getting shot, I thought to myself.

After Mr Wride and Steve had departed on their mission, I couldn't help wondering what kind of an ambush the pair of them could spring if a whole platoon of bandits suddenly turned up for their monthly ten minutes of joy. They were both people whom I really liked. David Wride was a tall, good-looking and very intelligent officer who possessed a rare ability to exercise authority without needing to raise his voice. Steve was a big, black Tamil from Ceylon. I always found him very pleasant and helpful, though sometimes of a rather simple nature.

I recalled how on a previous duffy after an all-day march, we had halted for the night in a Chinese cemetery. It was a clear night, so we decided simply to settle down among the gravestones wrapped in our poncho-capes. Before doing so, however, we sat in groups eating our conner. I was seated with Steve, Lightfoot and a couple of others.

As we finished eating, big, brawny Bob Lightfoot looked up at the sky and said: "It all looks very clear. That's really bad."

Steve frowned. "But surely that's good," he said. "It means it won't rain."

Lightfoot shook his head and then said solemnly: "A clear sky means a bright moon." He looked round at the surrounding gravestones and then added: "And the Chinese spirits don't like moonlight."

Steve gave a nervous laugh and said quickly: "Well, I don't want to hear about that."

"When there's a bright moon, the Chinese spirits rise up out of their graves," Lightfoot continued.

"Stop it!" Steve protested. "Don't tell me any more."

"The spirits get very angry because the moonlight has woken them up," Lightfoot persisted, warming to his subject.

"Oh, stop! Stop!" Steve pleaded, covering his ears with his hands.

Lightfoot now leaned forward and spoke louder: "And if they see a black man, he's the first one they go for!"

"Oh, no! No! No!" Steve exclaimed in genuine alarm, finally managing to silence the mischievous Lightfoot.

I don't know if the spirits did rise from their graves that night. The only thing that disturbed me in the middle of the night was the sensation of four little feet scurrying across my chest – presumably a rat or a lizard. Next morning, however, poor Steve looked very tired and drawn and I was told that he hadn't closed his eyes all night.

I will now return to the operation I was describing before. As our clothing remained pretty wet, we spent a rather cold and uncomfortable night. I awoke the following morning, relieved to find Mr Wride, safe and sound, stretched out on his poncho beside me in the basha.

"Good morning," I greeted him. "How did you get on?"

"What d'you mean?" Mr Wride asked defensively.

"The ambush last night," I said, a little impatiently. "Did any bandits show up?"

"Oh, no. No," Mr Wride answered. "We hung around for a few hours but nobody came."

He seemed very evasive and I now began to put two and two together.

After breakfast, Lance Corporal Joe Short took a patrol out while the rest of us just lazed around, most of us in our favourite position – flat on our backs. In one corner of the basha, Privates Goff and Jarman and two others monotonously sang at five-minute intervals:

"Glorious! Victorious!
One bottle of beer between the fourius.
Thanks be to God there aren't no moreius
'Cos one could drink the fucking lot himself!"

Nearby, some chaps were having a discussion about how it was better to be in 9 Platoon than in 8 because as one of them put it: "Crisp flogs his men."

This chatter was no doubt what prompted Mr Wride to turn his head and say to me quietly: "You know, Jock, when I was in D Company, I used to be out on patrol first thing in the morning and I used to keep going all day long. Sometimes I didn't get back till after dark. If I'd have kept that up, I was bound to have got a bandit sooner or later. I'd have probably got one before John Crisp did."

"Well, why didn't you keep it up?" I asked.

"I don't know," he said pensively. "I suppose I just got tired of pushing so hard."

Just then, Steve (the Tamil CLO) came over and crouched beside where Mr Wride and I were sprawled out on our poncho-capes.

"How are you feeling, sir?" Steve enquired.

"I'm OK," Mr Wride replied, sounding a trifle wary.

"Listen, sir," Steve said. "I think it's about time I had some leave. D'you think you could speak to the Major about it?"

"Well, I might do," Mr Wride answered with little apparent interest.

Steve now spoke in slow and very meaningful tones: "Would you like a cup of coffee, sir?"

At this, Mr Wride raised his head sharply and exclaimed: "That's blackmail!"

Steve laughed and Mr Wride now laid his head back again and said calmly: "Well, I might have a word with him if I can catch him in a good mood."

It was then that I became convinced that two and two definitely made four!

In the afternoon, Mr Wride took a patrol out and I went along as a rifleman. We searched a lot of hilly country which the jungle was reclaiming from the rubber. One slope was covered in the tracks of wild pigs that led to two muddy waterholes which were situated, strangely, on the summit of the hill. As we were wending our way down the other side through dense trees and undergrowth, I narrowly avoided bumping my nose into a large hairy-legged spider that was dangling from a vast web right in front of my face. Eventually, having found no signs of the enemy, we returned to base. After I had burned off half a dozen leeches that were bloated with my blood, I attempted to get my faulty wireless working but it was to no avail.

Next morning, however, I miraculously made wireless contact, without understanding how, and managed to arrange a transport rendezvous. We then packed up and made quite a fatiguing march to Junjong, from where two short patrols were sent out before our transport picked us up.

In the back of the 3-tonner as it sped on it's way home to Serdang, I gave amused consideration to the likelihood that Mr Wride and Steve would regard this operation as having been highly successful!

83.

Penang Joe

Redvers Battersby – Serjeant A Company

One person who must be mentioned is Joe Woodford, the manager of the Hotel Metropole in Georgetown, popularly known as "Penang Joe".

Joe was homosexual, but nearly all the Battalion knew him and whether you were that way inclined or not, you were always welcome at the hotel. You would always be sure of a good meal, a lecture on the bad girls and your taxi fare back to camp if you were broke. He

29. The grave of Private Hugh Kelly, an MT driver attached to B Company who was killed in an ambush on 3 December 1949. This photo was taken nearly a year later on All Souls Day, 2 November 1950. The grave at Western Road cemetery is replete with flowers from Penang Joe.

told me that he had adopted the KOYLI as they were a grand bunch of lads.

When there was a funeral – and we had a few – Joe always attended. Also, he looked after the graves and regularly put fresh flowers on them. In addition to that, he took photos of the graves for the bereaved folks back home and as far as I can recollect, he kept in touch with them afterwards.

His kindness should not be forgotten.

84.

Great Times

Chris Roberts – Private C Company

My Draft arrived in Penang around June 1950. We did a bit of jungle training and then went straight out to the mainland. Kulim camp was my first stop and my introduction to C Company which I stayed with from start to finish. I had some great times at Kulim. It was the best camp of all. I used to organise the Company's football activities. Once, I got into hot water when for one particular match I dropped CSM Allen from the team. My name was mud for a while after that.

I was in 9 Platoon. I can remember the signallers Jock Scurr and Swede Martin who were on a lot of duffies with us. It was no joke having to hump a wireless set up hill and down dale. I carried Swede's set once or twice, so I know the score.

A lot of funny things happened to me and my mates in Malaya, but what was funny forty-five years ago may not seem funny now. I can recall one duffy we were on during monsoon weather early in 1951. We had been out on patrol for about three days and were thoroughly soaked and fed up. One night in the pitch dark, my mate Roy "Ginger" Thomas suggested that we should obtain some shelter by crawling under a Malay dwelling. So we crawled underneath and it was like heaven being out of the rain at last.

We both fell fast asleep, not knowing that Ginger was lying under the waste pipe of the basha. Well, during the night while Ginger remained deep in slumber, it seemed like the whole Malay family must have soaked him with their sewage. When we awoke in the morning, I found it hilarious, but poor Ginger smelled of attar of roses for the rest of the duffy.

When we went on our next duffy, we did the usual patrolling during the day; then made camp, had our conner and finally settled down for a kip. Later on in the night, Ginger and I were wakened for stag.

We had only just got out of our bivvy and sat behind the Bren gun when we heard this loud noise of something coming through the undergrowth. It came closer and closer and passed within three feet of us. It was only when we came off stag that we found that whatever it was had gone straight through our bivvy. I had an old gas-cape that I used to hang over the end of the bivvy to keep our heads dry. Well, the bivvy was completely demolished and my gas-cape had disappeared.

When daylight came, we discovered from the tracks that the intruder was a wild boar – the only pig in the Malayan jungle to wear a gas-cape!

85.

Our Sweetheart

Jock Scurr – Private Signal Platoon

One evening in March 1951, when 8 Platoon had taken over from 9 on detachment at Serdang, I was alone in the Signals billet on the upper floor of the old planter's bungalow. Idly I tuned my "62" set to Radio Malaya and was delighted to hear the announcer introducing a half-hour programme of the hit records of Doris Day. Very quickly I activated my loudspeaker system in order to broadcast the music to the rest of the camp; then sat in front of the set to bask in half an hour of sheer enjoyment.

When the programme was finished, I decided to go down to the canteen for a drink. Hardly had I entered the door downstairs when a young soldier leapt to his feet from one of the canteen tables, bounded over to me and clapped me on the back.

"Jock," he exclaimed triumphantly. "I'm going to buy you a Tiger!"

"What for?" I asked in surprise, seeing that I only knew the chap casually.

"Because you got us half an hour of Doris Day," he replied as though he had just won the Pools.

"But I didn't even know she was going to be on," I protested. "I just turned the knob and there she was."

"That doesn't matter," he declared, quite unimpressed by my logic. "You got us Doris Day and I'm buying you a beer!"

So he did, and very nice it was too.

I have told this simple little tale in order to convey just how much Doris Day meant to the young servicemen of my generation. If Vera Lynn (a most lovely lady) was the Forces Sweetheart of World War Two, then Doris Day was unquestionably ours. Corporal Tom Morgan of A Company once went AWOL (absent without leave) just to see one of her films.

Although today's young people might find it hard to understand, Doris Day was revered as though she was truly the untouchable, virginal character that she always portrayed on the screen. Even the lewdest of lechers never said anything dirty about Doris.

86.

Grenades

Derrick Grice – Private Signal Platoon

While I was attached to D Company in April 1951, a grenade was thrown at some of our lads in the amusement park in Kulim. Four of our lads were wounded and so were some local people. I was on an outing in Kulim with Private Braithwaite, the medical orderly, when the incident happened. We decided to go straight back to camp. On the way there, a car passed us and one of the wheels must have hit a stone. But it sounded to us like a grenade-lever flying off. So we both hit the deck with our hearts in our mouths. This just shows how tense things were at that time.

There was another incident about a month later that I remember well. Underneath the raised-up bungalow in Kulim camp was accommodated the dining area, HQ sleeping area, arms cote and Signals billet. I had come in from a duffy and as usual had showered and cleaned my rifle and "68" set. After that, I was resting on my bed when there was a loud explosion. I felt as though I was lifted up off the bed and thought that we must be under attack. However, I soon learned that the cause of the explosion was a hand-grenade going off in the arms cote.

Apparently, a patrol had come in after ours and the men were handing in their grenades. The lads always carried grenades on patrol by clipping them onto their belts by the firing-lever. With this particular grenade, it appeared that due to friction whilst on the move, the lever had somehow worked loose from the pin and as the lad handed the grenade to the storeman, the lever flew off. The storeman hurriedly threw the grenade in a corner away from the ammunition and off it went.

Very surprisingly, nobody was injured apart from one of the lads who was lying on his bed next to the store. A piece of shrapnel seared a burn mark across his stomach. The Company Clerk, who was sitting typing in the office above, suddenly found shrapnel coming through the floorboards without him being hit.

I think that after this incident, grenades were no longer carried on belts in D Company.

87.

There's Only One Regiment

Jock Scurr – Private Signal Platoon

There was a portly CSM in HQ Company whose parent regiment was the King's Shropshire Light Infantry, of which he was very proud. When HQ Company was on parade in Minden Barracks, the CSM regularly scorned us with the contemptuous remark: "You Koylis are a shower! There's only one regiment and that's the KSLI."

Now it came to pass that in April 1951, a request was received from the KSLI in Hong Kong for volunteers from the KOYLI to make up their Battalion to full strength before its imminent departure to the Korean War. At the same time, the CSM received orders to join his parent regiment with the volunteer draft. Following this, the CSM was suddenly taken into hospital with suspected appendicitis and didn't recover until after the draft had departed. Then, a second order arrived urging the CSM to report to his regiment at the earliest opportunity. The CSM now suffered an unexpected relapse and returned to his hospital bed. However, about a week later, a communication arrived from the War Office approving the CSM's request to have his parent regiment changed to the KOYLI. The CSM now made an immediate and permanent recovery.

It seems that there was indeed only one regiment!

88.

A Detour Too Far

Ron Stringer – Private Signal Platoon

The impact on one's life of those years in Malaya is totally out of proportion to the time they occupied. It can sometimes seem that everything afterwards was an anti-climax. The story which follows typifies much of the effort, disappointment and humour of our sojourn in those times.

In the Kulim area in April 1951, 11 Platoon, D Company went out on a day-patrol led by Lieutenant Tim Green. I was the signaller. We were dropped off early in the morning on the edge of the jungle with orders to make a sweep through the area and rendezvous with transport at a particular map reference later in the day.

At first, all went as usual with Tim blithely and blindly leading us through patches of jungle, lallang and paddy. We continued tramping along behind him until we reached a village around which lazed a large number of water buffaloes. Tim, as was his wont, refused to go anywhere near the beasts and hastily led us off on a wide detour around the village. Eventually, we came to a jungle fringe reaching down from a hillside and as it was just after noon, we settled down to eat tiffen.

I suppose we had been there for ten minutes when we clearly heard someone chopping wood nearby. One of the scouts, a former DLI man, went to take a look. He soon scrambled back to tell us that we were,

155

in fact, dining about twenty-five to fifty yards from a small, occupied bandit camp!

Tim hurriedly conferred with the Serjeant and decided to launch a flanking attack. Off they all charged with me, carrying my "68" set, trying to keep up at the rear. I couldn't see a damn thing but heard a lot of shooting and shouting up front. Then the inevitable happened. I tripped over a root and the wireless set crashed against a tree, shattering valves.

As so often happened, the bandits disappeared into the jungle without us managing to get any of them. I was unable to raise base on my wireless to report the news or to confirm transport arrangements. To make matters worse, owing to the detour Tim had lost his way. Hours later, in the dark, we struck a road and found a telephone.

We later learned that there had been consternation back at base. It was feared that we had been ambushed and transport had been patrolling roads, hoping for some signs of life. When we eventually turned up, exhausted and frustrated, there was great relief all round.

Moral: If you go looking for a needle in a haystack, you may find it by accidentally sitting on it!

89.

Whit Takes a Dive

Peter Griffiths – Private B Company

This story centres around a tall, strong but slim guy by the name of Whitfield from the Oswestry part of Shropshire. In April or thereabouts of 1951, my Section went on a patrol from our base in Lubok Segintah. Serjeant Geordie Dee was our leader and the Section consisted of Charlie Walker who was armed with a silent De Lisle carbine, myself as Bren-gunner, two men with Owen guns, two with Stens and six riflemen with short jungle rifles. Sorry I can't remember all the names.

We had been on a long, silent march through the paddy and villages of that area of Kedah. We covered all types of country that day; very hot and very weary. At last, the time came to stop for lunch-break, strange to say, in the centre of a village. Jones Double 0 (so called from the last two figures of his Army Number) faithfully broke out the half petrol-can and brewed tea. The remainder of us lay resting but facing out in a ready-for-action circle with the brew in the middle.

Whitfield now found he had not packed his mug or mess-tin, so he had nothing to drink out of. He went around the lads asking each one for something to drink from but unfortunately, on this occasion, no one had anything spare. However, I noticed an old tin can resting on leaves on the ground in a peculiar square area which was about a foot lower than the general ground surface and all covered with leaves. I duly showed this to Whitfield and said: "There you are, Whit. Wash it in the stream, then scald it in the tea before you get your drink."

Most grateful for my suggestion, Whit promptly jumped into this leaf-strewn area and disappeared up to his armpits in human excrement! We helped him out but afterwards no one would go near him, even after he'd had a good wash in the stream. Geordie could not stop laughing and, parodying the old joke, exclaimed: "If Whit was shit, you'd be constipated!"

Although patrols should always be silent, occasional helpless laughter accompanied us for the rest of the duffy, but the smell was terrible.

I hope Whit will forgive this true story and accept it in the spirit that it was related. These KOYLI mates were the best I have ever had. I would love to meet them all again.

90.

Glorious Thursday

Robert Hunt – Private 19th Field Ambulance RAMC

My tale is set in Kuala Nerang, north-east of Alor Star, and the happening was repeated numerous times during and after May 1951. It took place on most Thursdays (pay day) when we weren't on patrol.

I was at that time attached to A Company and had two KOYLI mates who I think both came from Birmingham. Their names escape me but one was a corporal. The three of us used to go to the NAAFI on Thursday night and purchase a couple of crates of beer – either Tiger or Anchor. Then we would retire to the MI tent, play cards, sing bawdy songs and get gloriously drunk.

When my two mates were legless and couldn't get back to their own tent to sleep, I – being a decent medical orderly – used to put them on stretchers in the back of the Ford ambulance and let them sleep it off. Next morning, they would return to duty, well hung over but grateful for my hospitality!

91.

Lest We Forget

This poem was written by Corporal "Pecker" Green of D Company, sometime prior to his departure to Korea with the KOYLI volunteer draft in May 1951.

> In Malaya's dark interior
> Where conditions are inferior,
> The swaddies lead a primitive life,
> Full of toil and sweat and strife.
>
> With three days' rations on their backs,
> They recce hills and jungle tracks.
> Up, up they climb, then down again,
> 'Neath scorching sun and blinding rain.
>
> As night draws near they choose a site
> Where they can sleep and also fight.
> With poncho-capes and bits of string,
> They build their bivvies, then move in.
>
> Their evening meal is soon prepared.
> In twos for sentry they are paired.
> Then one by one they fall asleep
> As night draws on so dark and deep.
>
> After a night of two hours' stags,
> First on the list, of course, are fags.

"Who's got a fag?" is the oft heard cry.
"Come on, cough up and don't be shy."

Then after washing and shaving too,
They light a fire and make a brew.
And then is served a mealy paste;
It's porridge made with too much haste.

Then on they push as yesterday,
Scouring the jungle for their prey.
Sometimes lucky, sometimes not;
Their code is shoot – or be shot.

At noon they halt and make a brew
And smoke a well-earned fag or two.
Then after having had a rest,
On they push with new-found zest.

For two more days they carry on.
The days pass quick; the nights are long.
Their hearts are strong, they do not falter.
Their goal no man on earth can alter.

At last a jungle clearing's found,
And the jungle's chatter is soon drowned
By aero engines shrill and loud,
As Daks roar over strong and proud.

Fags and food, clothes and boots
Are dropped to them by parachutes.
And the only thing they don't supply
Is a pretty blonde with a wistful eye.

But even a girl is sometimes seen
In the still of night in a dream,
But what's the use of that, they say,
At break of day she flies away.

But even so there is always one,
Carried by every son of a gun;
Soiled by sweat and none too clear,
A photo of his sweetheart dear.

30. Men of C Company patrolling in the Kuala Kangsar area in 1949.

And though she may be far away,
He's dreaming ever of that day
When they will meet on England's shore,
Together again for ever more.

92.

Their Needs Were Great

Jock Scurr – Private Signal Platoon

In May 1951, I obtained a posting to HQ in Penang where I remained for six weeks before proceeding to D Company. The few chaps I was pally with in HQ were only occasional drinkers, so most nights I ended up drinking alone. Being a bit of a "loner" by nature, this presented no great problem but I nonetheless missed my mates in C Company.

160

Consequently, the weekend of 19–20 May was a joyous one. On the Saturday morning, well after CO's kit inspection, old Signals mates Eric Hann and Bill (Dickie) Downs arrived at HQ from D Company for a weekend "gigolo trip". It so happened that Matt Busby, my pal from 8 Platoon, was also in Minden Barracks at that time to undergo an RSM's Cadre. So, on the Saturday night, Matt, my cousin John Kitchen (QM's) and myself went to the AKC to see Errol Flynn in *Silver River* – which I had already seen ten times before! While we three enjoyed this innocent entertainment, Eric Hann and Bill Downs had rather a heavy night down town.

On the Sunday afternoon, Eric and I went down to the pool for a swim. Upon our return to the Signals billet, we found that Wally Reeves had just arrived from A Company to be fitted for his battledress uniform for going home. So that night, Eric, Bill, Wally and I seated ourselves around a table on the rear verandah of the NAAFI and had a most enjoyable booze-up. After a while, we were joined by a couple of other soldiers who knew Bill Downs and most probably were from D Company. As the ice-cold Tigers continued to lubricate our insides, the chat grew wilder and more hilarious by the glassful.

Consequent to one or two very ribald yarns, someone announced to the rest of us: "I went with an Indian bibby last night. She was really great! When she stripped off and I saw the size of her tits, I just couldn't wait to get hold of her."

"Oh, shut up!" exclaimed one of the nameless soldiers from D Company.

The first speaker ignored this entreaty and continued: "I just grabbed her and pressed up against her in the buff. And when I kissed her, I could taste the curry and rice!"

"For fuck's sake, shut up!" protested the nameless soldier.

"Then, I laid her back on the bed," the story-teller related, no doubt quoting from the latest Hank Janssen paperback, "and I caressed the contours of her nubile young body."

"Shut up! For fuck's sake, shut up!" repeated the nameless soldier, bending forward in his seat with his hands pressed to his groin as though in pain. "If you keep on, I'll have to go down town!"

Quite unmoved, the story-teller continued: "When I climbed onto her, I couldn't get it quite right at first. So I put a pillow under her arse and then I just . . ."

At that, the nameless soldier leapt to his feet and declared: "I've got to have a woman!"

The other D Company man, who had been listening quietly throughout, now stood up and said calmly: "I'll go along with you."

"Will we have to get changed?" the nameless soldier asked excitedly.

"No," the other answered. "We don't have to go down town. There's a woman down by the MT Park."

"Right!" exclaimed the nameless soldier. "You're on!"

The pair of them then turned and hastened away; the nameless soldier striding ahead as though his very life depended on it. The rest of us just looked at each other and then fell about laughing. Another round of Tigers was now demanded unanimously.

The following day, we all had whopping hangovers and Wally Reeves was put in the "nick" for pinching a towel from the QM's store while being measured for his BD. Eric and Bill departed for Kulim and I reported for duty in the wireless tower, having had a most entertaining weekend.

A week later, a friend in the Signal Platoon – whom I shall call Tim – returned to Minden Barracks from the British Military Hospital in Taiping. A month earlier, he had contracted primary syphilis and although now considered cured, he was under strict medical instructions to abstain from both alcohol and sex for a period of six months.

Chatting to me in the barrack-room on the day following his return, Tim told me: "I had a great time last night. I went down town, drank a couple of Tigers in the Broadway, then went round to see the bint who gave me the syph and beat her up."

"What?" I exclaimed. "You beat up a poor girl just because she gave you a dose?"

"Well, I didn't actually beat her up," Tim now said defensively. "I just slapped her around the face a bit."

"What happened after that?" I asked.

"I shagged her!" Tim replied.

93.

Charlie's Last Patrol

Fred Sparkes – Corporal B Company

A t the end of my two months posting to Singapore in charge of the Weapon Training Demonstration Squad at the FARELF Training Centre, I returned to Battalion HQ in Penang, prior to being demobbed. But alas, I was seen there by Serjeant Major Lawrence from my own B Company who informed me that I had my last patrol to do.

Reluctantly returning to the Company base at Lubok Segintah, it was nonetheless good to see my best mate Charlie Walker again. We had done our jungle training together when we first arrived in Malaya and had both been posted to 5 Platoon and always been billeted together in the same tent.

I could perhaps understand why I had to do my last patrol, considering my recent absence from the Company – but not Charlie. He had been on all the operations with never a miss. It was tempting fate to go on patrol on 20 May 1951 when we were both due to sail for home on the troopship *Dilwara* on 24 May 1951.

The patrol during that long, hot day had been uneventful when we finally pulled up for a rest. Charlie and I sat on the bamboo verandah of a Malay basha, laughing and joking and feeding boiled sweets to some "bintis" (Malay girls). We thought the patrol had finished, but Serjeant Dee now called out for six or seven men to accompany him up the track to a police post about a mile away.

I had always been a Bren-gunner on previous operations but because of my absence from the Platoon, had lost the Bren to someone else. Our small patrol set out with Charlie as leading scout. We were in quite open country but there was very thick scrub to the right of us.

We saw Charlie suddenly drop to the ground. He shouted: "This is the military!"

There was a reply: "This is the police!"

Charlie now rose from the ground. A sub-machine-gun opened up and caught him in the chest. The rest of us dived for cover. Private

163

Hicks landed on top of a commie and put two shots into him on the ground. All hell was being let loose. We could not see our assailants but were all firing at the smoke from their weapons.

Eventually, all was quiet and we had a look around. The bandit positions were very heavily blooded in three places. But my best mate was dead. I was absolutely gutted.

I had the honour of being Corporal i/c pallbearers at Charlie's funeral in Penang cemetery on 21 May. I was very proud but stricken with grief that I would be sailing home without him in a few short days.

I visited Charlie's grave with my wife in 1993. When I came home from that trip, I managed to trace his family through a Durham newspaper. Charlie's sisters were over the moon to hear from me after forty-two years and to hear that Charlie was so well remembered by his former comrades. We have corresponded ever since and meet each other once a year. One sad fact that I learned from them was that when Charlie's mum and dad received the War Office telegram notifying them of his death, a letter arrived from Charlie shortly afterwards telling them he would be on the troopship home on 24 May.

God bless Charlie.

94.

A Definite Set-up

Peter Griffiths – Private B Company

By May 1951, I had become somewhat settled into the task of patrols and was becoming stronger and generally more efficient. On the 20th of that month, the whole of 5 Platoon was on patrol under the control of our Captain. We had patrolled all day, passing through rubber and overgrown secondary jungle known as belukar. (Virgin jungle, not being overgrown, is easier to traverse.)

At approximately 4 pm, the Captain called a halt to settle down for the night. In a short space of time came the call: "With or without!" This meant the stew was ready for those who did not want "splom" – our name for when pom (powdered potato) was added to thicken the stew to a sticky mess that you could stand your spoon in.

31. Patrols had to be especially vigilant when marching on an open track bordered by dense bush.

As this happened, a local Malay walked furtively into our bivouac area and asked to speak to the leader. We accordingly took him to the Captain and Serjeant. The Malay told us that the local police station was only one mile up the track and the police wished to meet with us. He then ran off. Serjeant Dee was obviously concerned by this but considered that the man was probably frightened of us, which was not unusual. The Captain now asked Serjeant Dee to collect a small patrol and proceed to the police station. I was honoured by being part of Serjeant Geordie Dee's Section, so I went. I think the total patrol numbered seven men including our interpreter "Grandad".

Charlie Walker led the way up the track, carrying his silent . 45 carbine at the ready. He was followed by Geordie, then the interpreter, then myself with the Bren, followed by a man with a jungle rifle and two with Owen guns. After three-quarters of a mile, we came out of the jungle and into the rubber. Then, the inevitable happened. As we proceeded up a small incline in a natural valley, we were bumped.

The noise was horrendous. When rounds pass you close, they crack and bang in a terrifying way. For a very brief time I froze. I think everyone did. However, I soon got into a firing position, taking shelter behind a handy tree, and started letting off five-round bursts to the right. Grandad was crying alongside me and pleading: "Don't let them get me!"

I could see gunsmoke coming from behind a tree, so I fired straight through the trunk. And then the Bren gun's barrel fell off! I forgot all training, picked up the barrel by the flash eliminator and slammed it back into place, burning my left hand in the process. The firing now slowed down and I heard Geordie shouting: "Get the Bren up here!" I started to crawl towards him but looking up, I saw him standing up, so I ran to him.

Then a foreign voice shouted: "Stop firing! Police!"

Geordie yelled: "They are not! Commence rapid fire!"

When I reached Geordie, he bent over for me to site the Bren across his shoulder and told me to fire towards twelve o'clock. I did so just in time to see the remainder of the bandits disappear over a ridge. Geordie now called for us to retire, and suddenly we realised it was all over.

The upshot of all this was that it had been a definite set-up in which we had lost Charlie Walker, killed one bandit and wounded another whom they had carried away. The bandits had also taken Charlie's De Lisle silent carbine. Charlie had been hit twice by bullets after his death and from his injuries I would have thought the weapon to be useless anyway.

After the order to retire, only Geordie and I were left to carry Charlie out. We took turns; one carrying Charlie in a "fireman's lift" and the other carrying our weapons. We then returned to the site to carry away the dead bandit whose elimination I supposed to be credited to Geordie Dee. We found blood behind the tree I had fired at and also found my jungle hat with a splinter from the tree sticking through it.

Back at camp, I had to go before Major Doyle to give my account of the action. I found that Geordie had recommended me for the MM. The officers asked me if I would sign on but I said no, as I wished to return home to be married. I did not get the MM and neither did Geordie. The reason was never explained but I had not regrets – then! When asked to show my burns, I showed the other hand as I was embarrassed about forgetting my training.

We buried Charlie in Penang with full military honours the next day. I was the leading bearer.

After I'd been on two more duffies, the Battalion returned to England, but a small contingent of soldiers was transferred to the Ox and Bucks LI in Cyprus. I was one of these and I hated it. I missed the KOYLI very much and have not seen Geordie since.

95.

Forfeits

Jock Scurr – Private Signal Platoon

At my own request, I was allocated to D Company on 21 June 1951 to spend my last month there, prior to my return to Blighty. D Company was at that time stationed at Kulim; my favourite location and the area in which the Battalion had experienced a good share of its action.

One night shortly after my arrival, there was quite a gathering in the Signals billet which was situated beneath the Officers' Mess in the old planter's bungalow. Present were signallers Dickie Downs, Eric Hann, Ron Stringer and myself. I don't recall Derrick Grice being there; perhaps he was out on patrol. But also present were Roy (Doc) Guy, Norman Emery the MT driver, an Officers' Mess waiter called Ayres and two or three others. After a few Tiger beers had been consumed, someone suggested we should play a game of forfeits. (In order that no one named above should be embarrassed, I should like to make it clear that only some of those present participated in the game, while others were merely spectators.)

I can't remember exactly how the game was organised, other than that men took turns in asking each other general knowledge questions and anyone who gave a wrong answer, of course, paid a forfeit. The first penalty involved a man having to drink a glass of Tiger after his questioner had stirred it with his penis. The second required a man to have simulated sex with a photo of a naked woman that was hanging on the wall. But my story centres around two of the players whom I shall call Wilby and Sims.

In his turn, Sims asked Wilby to tell him the date of the General Strike and when Wilby gave the answer as 1922, Sims instructed him to stand still while he urinated upon him, directing his stream upon Wilby's shorts until his tank was empty. Wilby was clearly unhappy about this but nonetheless braved it out. After Wilby had changed his shorts, the game resumed and as the questions continued round the circle, Wilby kept pressing his hands to his groin and muttering loudly: "If only I can hold this in!" However, just as it was approaching his turn to ask Sims a question, he exclaimed: "It's no use. I can't hold it any longer." He then ran outside to urinate.

Upon his return, he pointed a finger at Sims and declared: "You're really lucky. If I'd caught you out on the next question, I was going go make you lie down on your back with your mouth open and I was going to piss down your throat!"

At this, Sims sprang to his feet and proclaimed adamantly: "I would have done it too! I would have done it!"

Wilby now asked his question: "Who was known as The First Englishman?"

Sims thought for a moment and answered: "Winston Churchill."

"Don't be bloody stupid!" said Wilby. "It was Hereward the Wake."

"He wasn't called that," Sims protested.

"Yes, he was," Wilby insisted and then turned to me for confirmation. "Isn't that right, Jock?"

Actually, I didn't have a clue whether Hereward the Wake had been known as The First Englishman or not, but not wishing to appear ignorant, I nodded my head and answered: "Yes, that's right."

Sims was daft enough to suppose that I would know and accepted that he would now have to pay a forfeit. Trying to think up something new, Wilby looked around the billet and his eyes alighted on the stencilling equipment that someone had been using earlier in the day to name and number his kitbag.

"Right!" Wilby announced triumphantly. "I want you to paint black and white rings round your knob."

"OK," Sims responded unconcernedly. After opening the two tins of paint, he picked up a brush and got to work. First, he applied a fairly broad ring of white, followed by a similar one of black. He made rather a good job of it, to the expressed approval of the onlookers. So pleased was Sims with his handiwork that he continued with another ring of white and yet another of black; for which he received a round of applause amid general hilarity.

After that, the game shortly petered out for want of new ideas and everyone settled down to drinking and telling jokes. At an opportune moment, I sidled up to Sims and said to him: "What are you going to do about those black and white rings round your dick?"

Sims shrugged his shoulders and replied: "Well, I expect they'll wear off in a couple of weeks."

"But what are you going to say to the MO tomorrow?" I asked.

"What d'you mean?" he said, frowning.

"Well, haven't you read Company Detail?" I said. "We've all got to parade after breakfast for a Free From Infection checkup!"

96.

Farewell

Roy Caldecott – Lance Corporal A Company

The last time I saw Maureen was in June 1951, three days before leaving Penang to go home. She was still working at the Piccadilly but now only part-time. I had been busy with having my uniform tailored, handing in this and that, visits to the MO and one thing and another. So that particular night, I thought I'd better go down town before it was too late.

At 7 pm, I was sitting on my usual stool at the bar. I had just managed to stop Maureen from pouring a brandy; she had already opened a bottle of dry ginger. I asked for a small Tiger instead. She looked at me a little puzzled. We talked. She told me again how much she and Hazel and Soo had enjoyed themselves at our Christmas party. Since then, I had been stationed at Alor Star, from where I had travelled to Penang whenever I could. We talked also of our one and only picnic on that marvellous beach near Sandycroft, seventeen months before.

How I wished we could have had a lifetime of picnics! The time was getting late. I knew what I had to do. I reached over the bar and from behind Maureen's left ear I took the flower she always wore there. She tried to stop me but she was too late. She knew what I was doing. When I asked her to turn her head, her eyes flashed defiantly. "No!" she exclaimed. "Oh, no!"

"Please," I begged. "It's the thing I have to do."

Slowly turning her head, she cried: "How long?"

"Two days after today," I said quietly.

I placed the flower behind her right ear. She was free.

Two days later, I was on the ferry crossing over to Prai. Beside me were Arthur, Nobby and some of the best mates I'd ever known, but at that moment I felt completely alone. I was looking back at the Clock Tower shrinking. A lump leapt into my throat; tears came to my eyes. I tried to blame it on the sea breeze, hoping no one else had noticed. But I knew it wasn't the breeze. Would I ever see her again?

Soon afterwards, we were on the train heading southwards. Three years of our lives had gone and ahead lay Singapore, the ship and home. My thoughts returned to my lovely Maureen and I mused that as long as she carried a dead wasp in her snuffbox, she wouldn't starve!

I now found myself smiling. I handed out fags to my mates and lit one myself.

"*Cede Nullis*, lads," I said resignedly. "It's a good motto to live by."

Epilogue

Those were the days we can never forget,
Creating the memories that stay with us yet:
Of duffies and booze-ups and bibies and mates
And porridge that's riddled with ants on our plates.
Of berets of green and Minden white roses
And men on the sick list, blobbing with doses.
Of Tiger and trishaws, the City Lights beckon.
"Let's have five bucks worth. What do you reckon?"
Of bugles at dawn and tents soaked by rain
And Bren guns and matchets and men racked with pain.
Of the dark jungle night, all hooting and shrieking,

32. The Battalion parading on the sports field at Minden Barracks on 1 August 1950 – A Company in foreground. Each man wears a white rose above his cap badge to commemorate the Battle of Minden fought on 1 August 1759.

> While lying in ambush, not moving or speaking.
> Of brew-cans and corned beef and curry and peaches
> And snakes and mosquitoes and blood-sucking leeches.
> Of the fifty-round bandolier slung round your belt
> And the mucker who died and the grief that you felt.
> Of the nights in the Broadway and sultry Loh Tow.
> What wouldn't we give for a look at her now?
> Of night guards and jankers and close-order drill
> And cookhouse fatigues; we remember them still.
> Of football and swimming, those days on the beach,
> Happily far from the RSM's reach.
> Of the buglers so smart at the head of the band
> And the Battalion behind at the CO's command.
> Yes, those were the days we can truly call great,
> The stories of which we've been glad to relate.
> The Yorkshire Light Infantry's tales have been spun.
> True to our motto, we yielded to none!
>
> J. Scurr

Appendices

Appendix A

Roll of Honour

The following officers and men of the 2nd and 1st Battalions, King's Own Yorkshire Light Infantry lost their lives while defending Malaya against the Communist enemy during the years 1947 – 1951.

Private D J Mayoh	D Company	Road accident	11 November 1947
Private J S Morton	D Company	Road accident	11 November 1947
C/Serjeant D Price	B Company	Tree accident	24 April 1948
Private J Foley	B Company	Tree accident	24 April 1948
Private J R Marritt	D Company	Malaria	31 May 1948
Private R Guy	B Company	Cooker accident	31 July 1948
Private J Elliot	D Company	Accidentally shot	6 August 1948
Captain D G Lock	B Company	Killed in action	2 October 1948
L/Corporal K Hutchinson	B Company	Killed in action	2 October 1948
Private A Dobson	B Company	Killed in action	2 October 1948
Private H Woodhouse (att. B)	HQ Company	Killed in action	2 October 1948
Serjeant J Gilpin	C Company	Scrub typhus	25 July 1949
Private R Gee	C Company	Road accident	4 August 1949
Private K Ward	D Company	Killed in action	9 November 1949
Private A Carter	B Company	Killed in action	3 December 1949
Private J J H Godfrey (ACC att.)	B Company	Killed in action	3 December 1949
Private H Kelly (att. B)	HQ Company	Killed in action	3 December 1949
Private J Mills (att. B)	HQ Company	Killed in action	3 December 1949
Private A McAdam	C Company	Appendicitis	? January 1950
L/Corporal J McGee	C Company	Gastro-enteritis	1 April 1950

Private R James	B Company	Accidentally shot	18 April 1950
Private W J Boden	D Company	Killed in action	10 June 1950
Private J E Gough	D Company	Killed in action	10 June 1950
Private C M Harrison	D Company	Killed in action	10 June 1950
Private D Jones	D Company	Killed in action	10 June 1950
Private R L Hall	D Company	Killed in action	10 June 1950
Private J K Hudson	D Company	Killed in action	10 June 1950
L/Corporal V Brown	D Company	Died of wounds	16 June 1950
2/Lieutenant D S Pyemont	D Company	Accidentally shot	9 July 1950
Private D C Hicks	C Company	Accidentally shot	24 October 1950
Serjeant W C Baddeley	C Company	Accidentally shot	21 November 1950
Private J Gregory	A Company	Accidentally shot	1 December 1950
L/Corporal J D Whitehead	B Company	Killed in action	26 January 1951
Private A J Fee	B Company	Swimming accident	21 February 1951
Private C Walker	B Company	Killed in action	20 May 1951

Company Losses

HQ Company	3
A Company	1
B Company	12
C Company	6
D Company	13
Total	35

173

Appendix B

Enemy Personnel killed for certain by KOYLI Patrols 1948–1951

	1948	*1949*	*1950*	*1951*	*Company Totals*
A Company	—	—	3	—	3
B Company	5	8	2	2	17
C Company	1	2	2	—	5
D Company	3	8	3	—	14
Annual Totals	9	18	10	2	Final Total: 39

Appendix C

Decorations and Awards to the KOYLI in Malaya 1948–1951

Order of the British Empire	Lt Colonel A B Brown
Member of the British Empire	Lieutenant (QM) B Marney
Military Cross	2/Lieutenant P L Richards
Distinguished Conduct Medal	Private B O'Reilly
Military Medal	Serjeant T R Chadwick Serjeant K Holmes Corporal M O'Brien
British Empire Medal	Bugle Major B Harbisher, MM C/Serjeant A Bland L/Corporal D Hall
Mentioned in Dispatches	Lt Colonel A B Brown Major J R Acock Major F M De Butts Major F A S Murray, MC Captain R G Davies, MC

Captain A M Davis
Captain A C Elcombe
Captain G H Hulme
Captain D S Sutcliffe
Lieutenant J H W Haddon
Warrant Officer II A Crossland
C/Serjeant F Dolby, MM
Serjeant G Allsop
Serjeant L T Bateman
Serjeant F Bell
Serjeant P C Firth
Serjeant S Haley
Serjeant K Hutchinson
Serjeant W H Sanders
Serjeant F L Thomas
Corporal R W Bellringer
Corporal J Forth
Corporal T Morgan
Corporal R Mould
Private R Birkett
Private W Lyness
Private Y Yeaman

C-in-C Certificate

Serjeant P C Firth
Corporal I Lewis
Corporal C McAllister
Private R Abernathy
Private J Chippendale